D1525288

PRAISE FOR *TREEHOUSE PERSPECTIVES*

"The stories . . . give us a glimpse of life as it might be, and can be, if each of us follows our heart." **John Tuck and Cheryl Francis, Author and Illustrator,** *Listen Up! A Comic Guide to Thinking, Acting, Feeling and Healing*

"This one really drew me in. Tina and Kirby have a style of writing which made me laugh at their wit, but also allowed me to associate closely to even their most somber anecdotes." **Niall Gillett,** *The Reporter*, **Belize City**

". . . a fascinating fusion of memories, diary entries and poetry as the Salisburys recall close encounters, everyday experiences, and their attempts to reconcile humankind with the natural world." *Inspired Times* **(U.K. magazine)**

". . . flowed well, easy to read, characters well defined like a novel." **Tom Carrel,** *Missouri River Break*

"Delightful adventure—enjoyed all the specifics." **Wanda Urbanska, author,** *Less Is More*

"Gives courage!" **Ken Damro, author,** *A Northwoodsman's Guide to Everyday Compassion*

"In addition to entertaining you this book will give you pause for thought, whether your favorite topic is travel, family affairs, exotic environments, adventure or (you) are striving to live more simply." **Tim Burmeister,** *The River Press*

". . . I thoroughly enjoyed reading this book—a job well done!" **H. Lee Jones, author,** *Birds of Belize*

CHANCE ALONG:

A WIND WORTH WAITING FOR

CHANCE ALONG:

A WIND WORTH WAITING FOR

CHRISTINA L. AND KIRBY G. SALISBURY

Biama
Books

Biama Books
475 Main St.
Floweree, Montana, 59440
biamabooks@gmail.com

ISBN 13:978-0615738086
ISBN 10:0615738087

Cataloging Data
Salisbury, Christina L., Salisbury, Kirby G.
Chance along: a wind worth waiting for
1. Adventure—Western Caribbean 2. Traditional Boat Building—Belize 3. Sailing—Belize Barrier Reef 4. Marriage 5. Politics—USA, Latin America, Belize 6. Nature—forest and sea 7. Memoir

Cover and interior design: Christina L. Salisbury
Cover photographs: Christina L. Salisbury
Text photographs by authors, except pages:
      35 Gary Rominger
      192, 291 Christie Juarez
      205, 303 G.R. Hammer
      257, 281 Andy Baker
      276 Karen Harvey
      277 Brian Holland
      297 Russell Salisbury
      311 Rachel Graham
Sketches by Christina L. Salisbury

Printed in the United States of America

*Some names have been changed to protect the innocent and the shy.

This book is dedicated to
writers of sea stories,
sailors,
boat designers, builders,
and particularly to:

Pete Culler,
Bud McIntosh,
Sam Manning,
WoodenBoat Magazine
and
Jim and Anna Gladstone

Contents
CHISELS, CHIPS AND CREATIVITY

SALTWATER, SAILING, AND SUNRISES

"I learned this at least, by my experiment; that if one advances confidently in the direction of his dreams, and endeavors to live the life which he has imagined, he will meet with a success unexpected in common hours. In proportion as he simplifies his life, the laws of the universe will appear less complex, and solitude will not be solitude, nor poverty, poverty, nor weakness, weakness. If you have built castles in the air, your work need not be lost; that is where they should be. Now put the foundations under them."

Henry David Thoreau

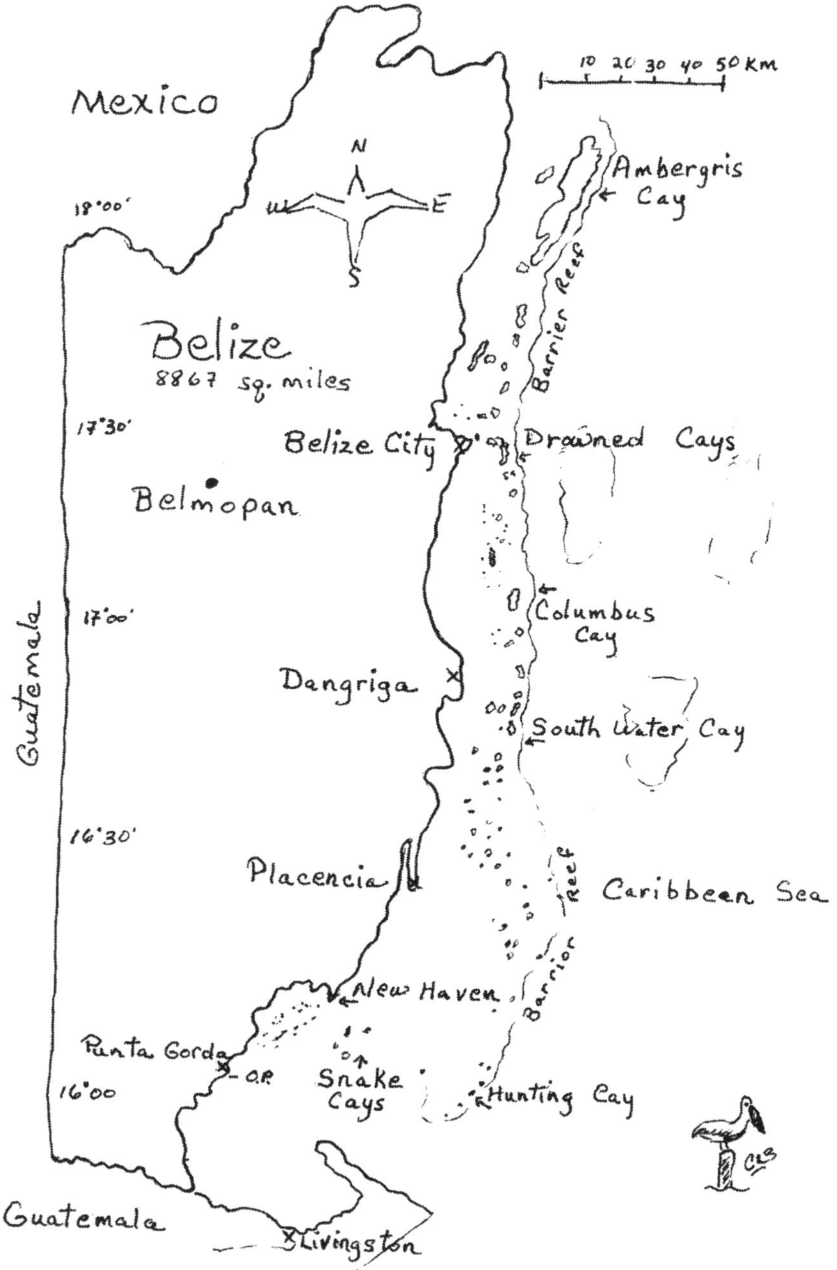

Mexico

10 20 30 40 50 Km

N

W   E

S

18°00'

Belize
8867 sq. miles

17°30'

Belize City

Belmopan

17°00'

Dangriga ×

Guatemala

16°30'

Placencia

New Haven

Punta Gorda

16°00   O.R.

Snake
Cays

Guatemala

S.Livingston

Ambergris
Cay

Barrier Reef

Drowned Cays

Columbus
Cay

South Water Cay

Reef

Caribbean Sea

Barrier

Hunting Cay

CHISELS, CHIPS, AND CREATIVITY

*"A wooden sailboat is like a living creature
and its construction must follow the
patterns that Nature prescribes." KGS*

1
~~~

January 1983

IT'S AN ILL WIND . . .

The wind reached a crescendo, and the rain whipped directly into our clearing. The waves crashed, the trees shook, and the ground trembled with thunder as the lightning struck closer and closer. This was one of the worst storms we had experienced at Orange Point and it was taking down some of the tallest trees. We were keenly aware of the fragile nature of our dwelling as the wooden frame vibrated and the plastic window shutters threatened to disintegrate. We prayed no branches would fall through our thatched roof. Breathing deeply, I tried to relax into an inner calm and ignore the raging elements. Gradually the wind started clocking around the compass as the mass of clouds moved on, and the forest became quiet with only the murmur of dripping leaves. Awed and relieved, we went back to bed and welcome sleep.

Early the next morning, we were up and out in the spreading sunrise to survey the damage. It was less than expected, yet the few trees that had gone down opened large gaps in the forest canopy as they pulled over or crushed smaller trees in their descent. It wasn't until we walked the shoreline that we saw the big bullywood that had supported our tree house, our first home in Belize, was also a victim of the night's storm. Over the years, waves had undermined her roots and the wind had at last thrown her down. Her root ball stood taller than our heads; her trunk lay intact thrusting 60 feet or more into the forest undergrowth. Twenty feet from the bare roots, we could rub our hands over the ridges in the bark where "U" bolts had clamped the support beams for the house. It was like losing an old friend, and for a bit we stood stricken. Memories surfaced and we began reliving those magical years we had spent in the protection of her mighty branches, now broken and twisted.

Looking for a way to test ourselves in the wilderness, we had built our home in this remote spot in 1972, trying to find a simpler life, one more balanced with Nature. We came to terms with the surrounding forest and sea and had found the degree of simplicity we could live with. We had survived gales of wind and rain, enjoyed splendid, sun-drenched days and magnificent, moonlit nights while raising our two children. Under the bullywood's spreading branches we started our wood craft business, and in her shade we rebuilt our little sloop *Morning Star*. In the tree house we had listened to the council of new-found friends (human and otherwise), come to terms with small spaces, extended our spiritual horizons and accepted Nature's rules.

The night storm had left the air crystal clear, and individual trees could be seen on the Guatemala Mountains fifteen miles across the bay. The creatures that had been living in the upper branches were scurrying around, adjusting to the abrupt 90 degree shift in their homes. Being much less adaptable and more fragile of body, we were glad we had relocated our home long before this event. There were obvious merits in knowing when to move on.

The downing of this forest giant reminded us that we each have our era, and the time for this old tree had run out. Our forest friend was prone, her solid trunk supported by the thick pads of humus that had fed her. She would now play a different role in the forest cycles; her decomposition would support new life. This event seemed symbolic to us; a phase of our life was also over and a new one had begun, one that we hoped would be sea oriented.

Sailboats became a part of our life after our first visit to Belize in 1971. *Tinker Toy*, the trailerable trimaran, came with us from California, serving as a camper on our trip through Mexico, as a sail trainer, and as a vehicle for our early explorations of Belizean waters. Owning the 15-foot sloop *Amigo* provided our teenaged son with a valuable experience in responsibility. *Morning Star*, 22 feet, carried rosewood from Golden Stream and Deep River to our craft shop on Orange Point. We used dories (dugout canoes) to go to and from our farming experiments on the Moho River and for general transport. Often we sailed the two miles into Punta Gorda on the early land breeze to do our shopping and then returned on the sea breeze as we trolled for dinner. We sailed for the pure pleasure of it, for the thrust of the wind, the feel of salt and sun on our faces, and the thrill of being at the mercy of uncontrollable and often unpredictable forces.

Over time we both began dreaming of someday building our own boat. My dream envisioned a self-reliant, sustainable life style. I could see it in my mind's eye: a sea breeze pushing us through white-capped, turquoise water in a boat big enough to live on comfortably and sufficiently sea worthy for our purposes, tools aboard ready to start work in the next harbor, plenty of provisions, books to read, good health and each other. Simply put—a life on the water called to me. For Kirby the dream of building a boat was largely the challenge of ultimate craftsmanship and the thrifty concept of using wind power. For both of us it meant being able to experience that particular bond with Nature that only sailing gives.

It was this silent vision that carried us through the hard and sometimes desperate times before our little craft business was going and it undoubtedly influenced the way the business developed. Though we started making wood items that demanded large stationary tools, we gradually narrowed our product line so only a small generator, portable lathe with band saw attachment, and some hand tools were required—tools that would fit easily into the cabin of a boat.

As the years went by, we struggled to keep the dream alive. In 1980 we decided to compromise by making do with what we had. *Morning Star* had served us well for three years but was in need of major repairs. We stripped her down to the deck beams and built her back with new decks, varnished cabin sides and laminated mahogany spars. I learned how to put canvas on decks, make sails, splice, and rig and to apply a variety of finishes. Kirby learned the basic skills of ship carpentry and joinery. Most importantly, we found satisfaction in working closely together on the same project.

Renamed *Sunalee,* she served as our transport when we distributed our craft items along Belize's 175 mile coastline. We found one or two gift shops in each tourist area that would stock our rosewood items. Delivering to them periodically was a requirement as well as a great excuse to make a sailing trip. Placencia, forty miles northeast was our favorite harbor, in part, because it was there our little yacht was noticed the most. The sea was everyone's front yard and they paid attention to the boats coming and going.

During one of our trips, we visited with Carolyn aboard her lovely Alden yawl, *Tane.* She was an experienced sailor who admired *Sunalee* and was willing to answer our questions about sailing larger vessels. "Don't worry about it," she said. "If you can take that little boat from one end of this country to the other, you'll find a 30-footer easy to sail in comparison."

In 1982, with both children gone and pursuing their dreams, our financial picture had improved marginally and we were finally on the threshold of the "big project." But before tying up all our resources (including travel money) for a period of years, we wanted to visit our families. We decided to treat the trip as a test to see if we were capable of making our little business portable and profitable at the same time.

Our old bus had transported our woodworking tools from Montana six years earlier. At various times it had carried lumber, logs, a horse and human passengers. We hoped it would make another long trip as a gypsy wagon. After a tune up, we loaded 1000 board-feet of mahogany, a dozen short rosewood logs, the chainsaw, generator, lathe, band saw and hand tools. Our small cottage industry, turning rosewood gift items, had become mobile. The question was: could we pay our way?

A pair of chests contained the tools, a two-burner stove, some pots and pans and our clothes. Foam mats on their tops were our beds, a pig tail bucket (five-gallon plastic), from the local store, held our water supply, and the bus steps became our bathing area. We traveled up through Mexico and into Texas where Kirby lathed in the shade of an orange tree near the Rio Grande and a pecan tree in Tyler. We sold lumber to boat builders in Galveston and burl tables to a gallery in Houston. In Wisconsin we set up shop in my parents' garage in Janesville and sold custom-made bracelets to their neighbors. We sold more lumber to Red Nimphius, a well-known boat builder, who lived and worked in a cow pasture. We made covered bowls on the family farm in Montana and plates in Dallas that we sold at a craft fair in East Texas.

Four months, several thousand miles and an engine overhaul later, we were back in Belize. We had paid our way around the United States with the lathe; our experiment was a success. The vision of doing a similar trip on the water was clearer than ever, and our enthusiasm was high.

I took one more lingering look at our tree-house tree, now at rest. We had arrived in a vulnerable state; this tree had protected and nurtured us until we had grown strong and confident in our new environment. We had outgrown the need for her security and moved on, expanding beyond her shade to shape our lives within the Belizean scene.

Placing a fallen orchid on her upper trunk where it might root again, I let the memories fade. After kissing Kirby's cheek, I turned back toward the house and the new shed—it was time to build a boat!

2

~~~

January 1983

IMAGINE THAT!

I remained sitting on the old bullywood as Tina walked back toward the house. She was as sad as I was to see the old tree down, but she took life's events in stride. It was a little harder for me.

We were embarking on a new enterprise many times bigger in every way than the tree house. Its construction took only six weeks, but building a boat was going to require a concentrated effort for several years. Not only would it require money that we would have to earn as we went along, it was going to require specialized skills I didn't yet have. Now that we had finally achieved some degree of living comfort and a modicum of financial stability, giving it up made me question the sanity of our new venture. But the underlying motivation was something we had little control of; my interest in building a boat had become a passion—a challenge that couldn't go unmet—and Tina was caught up in the vision of living aboard. She had the confidence that together we could make it happen, and she was probably right.

I glanced out at the sea, the source of our dis-ease, just in time to see Luke, a fisherman friend, paddling along the shore in his dory. "Mahnin', Mr. Kirby. Heavy breeze last night, no true?"

We discussed the weather and the loss of the thatch roof over his outdoor fire hearth during the storm. He would have to put it back in place before the next rains came or eat cold food. He hoped the storm waves hadn't driven all the bait fish into deeper water and thus out of the range of his cast net.

"Dat roof only big," he ventured, referring to the pole-framed shed standing near the back of our clearing.

"I am going to build a sailboat under it," I explained, and told him a little about it.

"I kin no 'magine' dat, but I wan' see it." There was a quiet moment in which we were both aware of the difference in our perspectives. With, "I gone look fu bait," he glided off toward the bight with a few deft strokes.

Luke, a Garifuna, was a dark-skinned man kept trim and muscular by his profession. His ancestors, a blend of African and Amerindian, had settled in the near-by town of Punta Gorda in the early part of the 19th century. Though Mayas were now moving in from the villages, the Garifuna still made up the majority of the town's population. His 16-foot dory might more accurately be called a dugout, since it was fashioned from a single log, but it was carefully designed, built to handle choppy seas, and was smoothly finished. With a simple flour-sack sail that he would raise when the wind was fair, a cast net, a paddle, and fishing lines he was in business.

After selling his catch at midday, he would have food for his family, a little bit for materials to repair the cookhouse, and maybe enough for a pint of rum. Today's evaluation would classify his business as sustainable and environmentally friendly. With just hand lines he wasn't going to deplete the fish stock, and everything he landed would be eaten, used for bait or released alive. I admired these men greatly: the simplicity and self-sufficiency of their trade, the honest pride it engendered, and that element of humility that only the sea can impart.

I mulled over the brief discussion I had had with him. I found this to be a good idea when cross-cultural conversations were involved. Often the same words had different meanings, and usually there were connotations that the words alone couldn't convey. In this case I was thinking about the concept of imagining. Did Luke mean he couldn't imagine *building* the boat or that he couldn't form a mental *image* of the boat? His people were intelligent, skilled and certainly not short on imagination, so what did he mean?

Luke's culture was based on mutual aid and sharing. History shows that those who can live in close cooperation with their neighbors have the best chance of surviving difficult conditions. Certainly the Garifuna had survived centuries of hard times, and as long as their culture keeps them working as a unit they will survive many more. But there are rules that must be followed to remain part of the group and every culture is restrictive at the same time it is supportive. His culture discouraged individuals from starting imaginative enterprises since they might disrupt the general equality required to keep unity.

We came from a culture where innovation was generally respected and rewarded, so our imaginations were supple though our skills in living in close community had never developed. In coming to Belize we found ourselves living without the support of a culture; at the same time we were free to pursue our dreams. Being able to visualize both the process and the product are essential first steps toward fulfillment.

On my way to the house, I passed by the lumber shed, a lean-to attached to the back wall of the shop. To the unprejudiced eye the open-sided shed contained rough lumber in a pile ten feet wide, six feet tall and twenty feet long. The layers of boards were separated by thin strips of wood that allowed air to pass through. The wood ranged in thickness from one-inch planks ten to twenty inches wide, to seven-inch beams fourteen inches wide. Lengths were from five to twenty feet. Colors ranged from off-white to deep purple. But to me, they weren't just boards; each piece had an identity and together they had served as tangible hope that our dream could someday be realized. Those boards had indirectly come from one boat, and I hoped to fashion them into another.

Back in 1976, we had been in Belize for four years. Our original nest egg had been depleted during the first two, and the earnings from a stateside, summer job were almost gone. We were spending precious resources maintaining the little Piver trimaran we had trailered down from California and were finding little time to use her. With mixed emotions, we put up notices: *Tinker Toy* was for sale. One of the first persons to ask about her was a tall, lean Texan.

Melvin, Clara Mae, and their two, teenaged children had left their west-Texas farm in the hands of a partner and had come seeking adventure and fortune in Toledo's Golden Stream area. They had agreed to manage the development of a large tract of land for a group of San Antonio investors. The colonial government considered clearing the forest as synonymous with development and made it a requirement for the purchase of any large tract. Field crops and pastures were to follow. So Melvin arrived with an assortment of well-used equipment, including a 48-inch circular sawmill from a past era. He was to finance the clearing by first logging out all the saw timber. Profits were to be shared with the owners.

Melvin had no experience with sailboats but thought *Tinker Toy* could serve as a good family getaway from the ranch. He wanted to try her out, and we planned an outing. With two families of four and Melvin's elderly mother and aunt we were over-crewed for little *Tinker Toy* so Melvin borrowed a big dory. We left Orange Point on the morning land breeze for a picnic at Moho Cay, 7 miles to the northeast. After a nice lunch under the palm trees, Melvin and I took the trimaran for a spin around the cay (island). It was soon apparent that his skills lay more with vehicles that had steering wheels and would go in any direction you wanted. Additionally, he felt naked being barefoot; but I couldn't allow his sharp-heeled, cowboy boots on the thin plywood decks, even though he showed me the rubber soles and explained they were "Texas Topsiders."

We were still several miles from home when Dark drew her curtain. We were sailing comfortably on the jib when we realized we could no longer hear the putter of the outboard on the dory. Melvin and the kids had been staying a couple hundred yards behind us. After receiving no response to our shouts, we dropped the sail, pitched the anchor and started doing our best to calm Mother. Her suppressed fears of the whole Belizean experience surfaced; she just didn't know why her Melvin J. was doing all these dangerous things down here in this foreign country. Though we had considered that question about our own motivation many times, we were still unable to give her a simple answer—if, indeed, there was one.

With flashlights and yells we were eventually re-united and we towed the dory and crew back to Orange Point. Apparently Melvin had hit a coral head, and the Seagull outboard had jumped "clean off the back of the boat." Melvin claimed the engine just kept going, and he couldn't paddle fast enough to catch it. He reckoned it was still going yet. Purchase of *Tinker Toy* was never mentioned again, but we had become friends, and he said that if we ever wanted lumber, he would be glad to cut it.

Eventually we sold the sailboat to a Peace Corps volunteer who was assigned to one of the northern cays. For the first time in several years, we had a bit of cash in our pockets, and we knew if we didn't set it aside for a worthy project it would gradually get used up for our everyday expenses. We had several worthy projects to choose from, but the one highest on the list (and the most foolish, considering our financial status) was the building of a boat.

A few months before we had received the plans for a 33-foot sailboat and I had prepared a complete materials list. Surprisingly, the $750 from the boat sale would buy almost all the wood it would take for the basic hull. We did some further calculations and decided if we worked another summer in the States we could spend the *Tinker Toy* money on boat lumber and still scrape by. We told ourselves the lumber was a wise investment; we could always sell seasoned boards for more than we had paid for the green ones. In reality we had been bitten by the boatbuilding bug and the only cure was to go through the process. That was how I found myself driving, every few days, the thirty-five, rough miles to Melvin's sawmill.

The reference books I had on boatbuilding woods were of limited use since they rarely discussed tropical woods. In addition to being dissimilar species, a much different product results when trees grow the year around. The characteristics that make wooden boats last in the tropics differ from those best for boats used seasonally in colder conditions. I made it a habit of talking with Belizean boat builders whenever I had the chance. Often the discussion was about the best woods to use for the various parts of the boat and their availability, so most of my choices of wood varieties were based on local knowledge. Fortunately, Melvin's ranch was in a transition zone at the edge of the pine savannah; it had a mixture of terrains and soil types, and each of the species of wood I had chosen was available.

Santa Maria (*Calophillum brasiliense*) is one of the most versatile of Belizean woods. The tree produces a large-diameter, straight bole and is common throughout the coastal plain of Belize. Its wood is quite durable, of medium density and strong. It is as pretty as mahogany but its wavy, interlocking grain makes it difficult to finish and it tends to twist and warp while seasoning. I decided to use it for the thick timbers that would make up the centerline and for athwart-ship beams.

Pine (*Pinus caribea*) is one of the few coniferous trees in Belize. It is much denser and more resinous than the northern pines I was familiar with. The resin keeps water from penetrating and makes it long lasting and marine borer resistant. Its grain is straight; it has few knots, it seasons well and was my first choice for the hull sheathing.

Honduras Mahogany (*Swietenia macrophylla*), often mimicked, never duplicated, is a wonderful wood to work. It seasons well, is straight grained and available in wide, long planks. It is a fast-growing tree in southern Belize. It is not particularly durable in tropical climates, nor is it compatible with galvanized fastenings, but combined with rosewood, it would make a beautiful cabin interior.

Black Cabbage Bark (*Lonchocarpus rugosus*) is one of the most durable of Belizean woods. Its high density limits its use to the lower parts of a sail boat. I planned to use it for floor timbers and for the rudder.

I would arrive at the mill in my spring-less, old Land Rover, feeling as if I had been practicing cannon balls in a wading pool. With tape and lumber list, I examined all the logs recently arrived in the mill yard. Jose, the foreman, would come with his big chain saw and buck up the logs to the right lengths. A wheel tractor dragged them to the ramp where they were rolled by hand onto the carriage. On the fresh cut ends, I chalked the cross sectional profile of the timbers I wanted, avoiding sapwood and heart cracks. The little mill grunted with the biggest logs and we would have to keep adding water to the radiator until the job was done. Melvin gave me a chance to accept or reject the lumber as it flipped over onto the out-feed rollers. No boat builder could have asked for better terms. When our trail was dry enough, I borrowed Melvin's old truck and brought that glorious pile of lumber home to Orange Point.

Bringing my mind back to the present, my nose sorted through the mixture of scents: salt air, humus from forest decay, and wood smoke, until it settled on freshly-cooked pancakes. At that point my salivary glands took over. As I walked quickly to the kitchen, I decided I had probably over-analyzed the recent discussion. Luke couldn't imagine building a boat like I had described, but left unsaid out of politeness, was the thought that he couldn't imagine why anyone would want to build such a boat. It would take years and lots of money; his dory was just right for his needs and the maintenance of a bigger boat would be overwhelming. It was likely as simple as that.

In our case, I could visualize the boat that would help fulfill Tina's dream—boundless horizons for our home which could be moved at will using an unlimited fuel source and a mobile business that would make us financially self-sufficient. We had developed the business and, with our trip in the old bus, had proven its mobility. It was evident from our front porch that the horizon was still unrestricted and the fuel source was blowing through the window at about 15 knots. Only the moving home that could take advantage of it all was missing; that was where my role in the creative process came in. Imagining it was not at all hard—putting it into a physical form was the challenge now. I poured on the brown sugar syrup and tucked into my pancakes.

3

~~~

Spring 1974

A KETCHY DESIGN

Building a good boat, like most creative projects, requires having a specific design in mind. The one we chose was decided in a process that spread out over several years.

Back in 1974 we were in the cockpit of Mark's 32-foot trimaran on the Rio Dulce in Guatemala. The night was calm and the air balmy. Mark had his audience of eight enraptured. We heard how he started his circumnavigation from California, the huge fish he caught on his way across the Pacific, the near miss with a freighter at night, and now we were in the midst of his third hurricane. He played an audio tape of the dramatic climax to the storm, his shaking voice accompanied by a screaming wind and crashing seas. "The key to surviving hurricanes," he concluded, "is to have a boat fast enough to get away from the eye."

As we began to relax, John, an ocean sailor himself, commented quietly, "Personally, I try to avoid hurricanes."

The next day we had started back down the river with *Tinker Toy*. The wind was calm but the current was in our favor, and the tiny Seagull engine loafed along. We entered the spectacular canyon in the lower river with its four-hundred-foot, nearly-vertical cliffs and its abundance of aquatic birds. We spent the night in Livingston harbor and by first light had started the 16-mile sail back to Punta Gorda.

Our first sailing trip to a foreign country had been exciting and educational. We had learned that three portly Guatemalan officials can sink a small dinghy, and that sailing up the "Rio" against a strong current is nearly impossible, but more importantly, that boats are made according to certain designs, and the designs vary greatly depending on the intended function of the vessel. Mark chose a trimaran for its speed. Excitement was its reward. John sailed a ketch, built stoutly enough to survive most anything and heavy enough to carry a year's provisions. He sacrificed speed for security. As with most of life's endeavors, we were learning boat design was about compromise.

I loved the concept of traveling on water, and I could fantasize how it all started. Somebody's cave was flooded and he found himself being swept down the river clinging to a drifting log. He eventually managed to get astride, but the current still took him out to sea. With his flint knife he cut the leaves off his drifting tree, plaited them together, and when the sea breeze came up, his rudimentary sail carried him back to shore. In Belize logs were still being used as boats but shaping them had become a sophisticated procedure. Each boat was specifically designed for the job that it was expected to do, where it was to be used (river or sea), and how it would be propelled. The resulting "dories" were efficient in carrying cargo and passengers.

The experiences with our various boats had been informative and our learning curve was steep. The quickness of the trimaran kept us alert. With most of the three hulls above the surface, she had a lot of windage and her own mind as to where she wanted to go. Raising anchor and getting off on the right tack was always a challenge. Kirby would raise the sails while I took the helm, and Scott stood ready to "back" the jib. Hand over hand Kirby would pull in the anchor line, trying to keep the bows a few degrees off the wind in the direction we wanted to head. With luck, patience and coordination it would work, but once in a while a gust would sweep the bow the other way at the last moment, pulling the anchor out, and away we would go toward shore or shoal, praying she would respond to the helm before we struck.

Tinker Toy always came about at the last instant but the anxiety was a bit much, and we never really felt confident she would answer the helm as needed. Occasionally something would fall overboard (a dog or fishing pole), complicating the already tense moment and adding to the confusion and excitement. Off the wind in a heavy breeze, she would get up on the waves and surf. Whew! Who needs to cross oceans for thrills! It was certainly exciting and Mark would have loved it, but for us the thrill quickly wore off once we realized we had very little rudder control under those conditions. We decided speed was not our goal.

Though only a fraction of the size of John's big ketch *Coryphena,* Scott's sloop *Amigo* shared the characteristic of being a displacement hull, that is, she was destined to spend her life in the hole she created in the water. She would never get up on the surface and plane like a trimaran.

On the way to town one day, we became becalmed. We needed to get Kirby's visiting aunt and uncle to the airport in time for their flight and asked a fisherman with an engine to give us a tow. As our speed through the water increased, so did the size of the waves on the bow and stern until they were level with the deck. Essentially we had dug a hole in the water by towing *Amigo* beyond her hull speed. Had we continued we might have been pulled under the water's surface. The experience was a fine example of the speed-limit principle for displacement hulls.

Though she traveled slowly, *Amigo* could carry a tremendous load for her length and width, whereas, *Tinker Toy* had to be kept light to be able to perform properly, her outer hulls barely touching the water. To keep her to a minimum weight, she was constructed of thin plywood with an outer layer of fiberglass cloth.

A few months after getting back from Guatemala, *Tinker Toy* broke loose from her mooring and ended up a mile away on a rocky shore with the bottom of the main hull ripped out. We refloated and towed her home where Kirby rebuilt her, making her stronger than the original. It was an expensive repair since all the materials had to be imported. As Kirby crawled out from under the repaired hull, arms itching from fiberglass dust and sand fly bites, he vowed that the next boat would be built with solid lumber. Lightweight trimarans were out of the question.

In his quiet way, John had convinced us of the seaworthiness of *Coryphena*. She had been built with traditional materials, most of which would be readily available in Belize, and with the same basic techniques that Belizean builders used, plank on frame. He said the designer, John Hanna, had drawn a smaller sister to her called the Tahiti Ketch. The fact it was designed for amateur builders would be to our advantage. Our own vague ideas of what kind of sailing we would do came from long discussions when we were visiting my aunt and uncle (who were building their second boat), the voyagers we met, and from reading sailing books—all written by couples who had lived aboard and made long ocean voyages: the Hiscocks, the Griffiths, and the Pardeys.

With hardly a copper in our pockets, we were caught up in the dream. Then a magazine arrived from Uncle Jim, and amazingly it had a picture of a Tahiti Ketch on the cover, a story about its seaworthiness, and an address for the designer. We sent off for the building plans for the modest sum of $10. When they arrived Kirby pored over every detail. In his mind he assembled the boat and knew the dimensions of each timber, frame and plank and what fastenings and tools he would need to actually build it. It was his way of dreaming—mine was to visualize where such a vessel could take us.

The lumber to build the Tahiti was acquired when we sold *Tinker Toy,* but we were far too busy earning a living and raising a family to start building. Still, without a road to the Point, boats were our primary means of transport and therefore part of our daily lives. As it turned out, the several-years delay of the boat construction was fortunate. Our initial choice of the Tahiti Ketch model was based mainly on the fantasy of ocean sailing. But experiences in

Sunalee and the feedback from long-range sailors started revealing the kind of sailing we would most likely be doing.

Belize's coastline is protected by a barrier reef and inside it are several hundred cays. We enjoyed exploring each cay we came to, its anchorages and its surrounding reefs. We loved to get up in the wee hours and catch the light offshore breezes and sail by moon and starlight. We would usually be tucked into a snug anchorage by late afternoon. Our craft business was modestly successful and distributing rosewood orders by water was fun. We envisioned continuing to do so while living aboard someday. We realized it was a coastal boat we were looking for, not one for ocean voyaging. We made up a list of the design characteristics we wanted:

1. It must resemble traditional Belizean boats in method of construction, materials and general shape, to allow building, maintaining and repairing with local resources and equipment.
2. It must sail well in light breezes and should have reasonable windward performance.
3. It must have a draft of less than five feet.
4. Two cabins were needed, one for living and one for work.
5. It must utilize the lumber we had on hand, so it could be no longer than 30 feet on the waterline or more than 11 feet in beam (width).

The Tahiti scored about 80 out of 100 when put to the test. Her failing was in her performance. She was noted for her ability to cross oceans safely in the toughest of conditions, but she sailed poorly to windward and didn't do well in light breezes. Now that we knew what we really needed we started looking at design catalogs in earnest, and we began a careful study of local boat construction.

At the upper end of Placencia village, a schooner in the forty-foot range was at anchor. She was much bigger than the local smacks and had the look of many of the vessels we had been studying. Kirby was talking "boats" with a fisherman cleaning his catch near the co-op.

"What about that dark green boat anchored up in the cove? Is it a local boat?"

"Yeah, man, she for Mr. Nick. She built in the City. She's a nice bo't and sail j-u-s-t fine. You find the gentleman der, where she anchored."

Eagerly we started down the two-foot-wide sidewalk that served as Placencia's Main Street. A half mile up the walkway, we found Nick, his wife Lou, and their young daughter. Their octagonal house was designed by Nick, a talented artist with an eye for the unusual, but his 40-foot schooner, *Miss Lou,* with her bottle green hull and buff decks, was as traditional as they come.

Nick designed the *Miss Lou* himself, but had been influenced by the schooners of New England designer Robert "Pete" Culler. We had read some of Culler's articles in the *Mariner's Catalogs* and knew about him as a respected boat builder, but we weren't familiar with his designs.

Choosing a *boat* design was new to us but the concept was not. A college degree, an industrial job, a house in suburbia, a station wagon and a mortgage—those were the components that defined our early marriage; we lived according to the popular design of the time. After practising that lifestyle for several years, we were able to determine what our real goals in life were. We had arrived in Belize seeking a new and more appropriate design—for living.

When the sea was rough, the one-mile-long trail gave us access to town, groceries, friends, and mail. The family crowded around me as I appeared out of the forest with a load of groceries in a backpack and a couple of bags hanging from my shoulders. Communication was a cherished part of our lives. So while food was essential, it was likely to be the mail they were most interested in. I passed over the packet where they each found a letter and handed the remainder back. I went into the house and dumped the backpack and bags on the floor. After washing my sweaty face, I put the kettle on and went out to the front porch hammock. Kirby followed.

I soon spied a design publication by the *National Fisherman Magazine* Nick had promised to send. On page 19 was a story about the building of the *Miss Lou* which we read avidly. While talking about it over our tea, I glanced at the adjoining page. The headline was *Simplicity, Economy Shown In 33' Culler-Designed Ketch.*

As I read on I became excited. The specifics of the design seemed to suit our situation: it was of moderate draft, the generous beam would make her stable, and the fine entry and easy lines would allow her to perform well in light airs. She was inside ballasted, nicely ventilated, with the expectation that the boat would be simple and economical to build and maintain.

The right size—even two cabins! Of course, we couldn't know how she would perform ahead of time, but she was designed for coastal use and was described as "easily driven." We wasted no time in sending for the plans. A few weeks later they arrived and Kirby immediately started measuring. Yes, our timbers should serve nicely. The hull was obviously finer in the ends than the Tahiti and his calculation of the prismatic coefficient indicated she would sail better in light conditions.

Voila! We had hit the jackpot. Culler's philosophy of simplicity, old time and well-proven materials and gear struck us as particularly appropriate to our Belizean setting.

It was the working craft heritage, a combination of beauty and utility, that most appealed to me. We admired the functionality of the Belizean fishing smacks and sand lighters and the stories of the old trading schooners of these waters. Such schooners worked the coastline of the western Caribbean: Honduras, Guatemala, Belize, and around to

Campeche, Mexico, delivering their cargos along the Gulf Coast of the United States. In our local waters they loaded timber and sugar in Port Honduras. The skills needed to work this reef-strewn shore were of the highest order. I was pulled to take up this challenge. Sail power was still the most efficient use of the natural resources and satisfied my soul's need for romance.

Quite some years before, I had come across a photo of a lovely schooner. I had cut it out of a magazine and put it up on the wall behind my kitchen sink. It served as a prompt to whisk my thoughts into pleasurable channels while doing dishes. She did not have a fancy pedigree like a Herreshoff or an Alden but had very pleasing lines. Her rig was traditional and she was dressed mostly in paint with only a small touch of varnish here and there. She had a personality that spoke to me in her working woman sort of way.

When I first saw Pete Culler's drawing of "our" ketch, it evoked the same feelings and it prompted me to examine the photo in more detail. With magnifying glass, I could just make out the boat's name, *Integrity*. Wow! I had had a picture of Pete's most famous schooner on my wall for years!

Nick's endorsement of Culler, the appearance of the *National Fisherman* publication with what appeared to be the perfect design for us, and the special affinity I had for his boats, all combined to give me the feeling we were being led to a specific destination. We had only to follow and sail on into the complex and sometimes murky waters of boatbuilding.

4

~~~

February 1983

LOFTY IDEALS

I shut off the little generator, took off my scarf, mask and earplugs and walked out of the work shop for a stretch in the balmy sunshine. It was midmorning, and I had finished my day's quota of lathe work. The little shop building had already served as a horse barn and its loft as Christie's bedroom. The craft business had replaced our farming experiments, and my lathe now stood where we once had a manger for the milk cow.

Woodturning is a craft which is sometimes used for artistic expression. I considered myself a craftsman, not an artist, but I was very particular about the shapes and curves I carved into our items. Our customers chose pieces for a nice feel and attractive curves, rather than for function. That made sense to me. I liked to tell Tina that I had quite rationally chosen her for her intellect, but certainly the above-mentioned characteristics weighed heavily in her favor.

We had been in Belize four years before we had found a way to make a living. We had simplified our life style, and our farming efforts provided a portion of our food, but educational supplies for the children, books and occasional travel required cash that subsistence agriculture could not provide. With the proceeds from our second summer's earnings on my brother's Montana farm, we bought woodworking tools and started the craft business immediately upon our return. My skills at the lathe grew steadily, and as our orders increased, Tina began doing the finish work, a task that required as much time and skill as the shaping. We offered a large variety of gift items of guaranteed quality and we strove to fill our orders in a timely manner.

I was working on a large order of rosewood items for a missionary in the western district. It was his practice to give a token of appreciation to each of his supporters. KirbyKraft had received some notice as being the producer of unique products. The previous week we had been commissioned by the Catholic parish to make "a suitable gift" for Pope John Paul who would be making a brief stop in Belize during a whirlwind tour of Central America. Because rosewood is so dense, we were accustomed to crafting tableware not normally made from wood, such as teacups, coffee mugs and wine goblets. I had hoarded a piece of rare rosewood burl, and I used it to turn a chalice and matching paten. Tina had done an especially nice job of finishing them. The gift was to be presented that afternoon at the international airport in Belize City.

After a little wash up at the water vat to get the dark red sawdust and chips out of my ears and beard, I stepped up onto the boat-shed floor. The gabled roof structure of poles from our forest and corrugated tarpaper panels started 11 feet above the 20 by 40-foot, wooden floor which was 30 inches above the ground level. Without walls, there was plenty of light, but by mid- June, a few months' time, the rainy season would be in full force and plastic drop curtains would need to be fashioned to keep the water out.

Backed by the ever-encroaching forest, the new building adjoined the workshop which was twenty-five yards from our seaside, two-storey, thatched house. The buildings were centered in a one-acre clearing that had been planted in coconuts and fruit trees. Scattered about were some large hardwood trees, like the cabbage barks that shaded the house and the big bullywood that loomed over the boat shed. With the sea always within sight and hearing, it was an inspiring venue for boatbuilding.

I was in the process of lofting, and after a month's work had yet to produce anything that would become a permanent part of the boat. In wooden boat construction, the lofting process is the final stage before beginning to saw boards and pound nails. Pete Culler probably started the design process by building a wooden model scaled at a half inch to the foot, or one twenty-fourth the size of the actual boat. Measurements from the model would have been used to produce the lines on the plan. He had taken a three dimensional model and reproduced it as lines on a two dimensional piece of paper. His goal was to transfer information that would allow a builder to produce a full-sized boat exactly the shape of his model.

To assist the loftsman, the designer measures his own drawings, scales them up to the full-sized measurements and lists them in a table of offsets. Unfortunately his measurements can't be made precisely; whether he measures to the inside of his pencil line or to the outside can make a significant difference when scaled up by a factor of twenty-four, and without correction these irregularities will be introduced into the structure itself. Even if the builder can esthetically tolerate these bumps and low spots, the thick planks will not conform to an uneven framework.

Using the table of offsets, the loftsman reproduces the designer's lines onto the loft floor and by bending a long strip of wood along each line and adjusting it into a fair curve he corrects the inherent errors in the table of offsets. The measurements taken directly from the loft floor are used to fabricate the full-sized molds. In one critical step, design has evolved into a tangible construction pattern.

I had an additional step to perform because we had not purchased a complete set of plans. Apparently Pete had been commissioned to draw up a proposal for a specific client, and that is what we had purchased—the final design plan having never been completed. The proposal lacked many of the features a complete plan would have, including the table of offsets. When the drawings arrived I eagerly measured the designer's lines and produced my own table. My promptness saved me some real headaches. With our tropical humidity, the large sheets of paper the lines were printed on swelled over the next few months, and the expanded drawings would have produced a boat several inches longer than intended. The extra work of completing the plans was counterbalanced by the thrill of knowing ours would be the first boat built to this design (as far as we know, it is still the only one).

Until the last couple of days, the process had gone smoothly. That was in part due to previous experience at lofting in the church. We had spent the summer, seven years earlier, working for Russ, on his Montana ranch. We were already hooked on the boatbuilding idea, and most of our summer's earnings were being spent on woodworking tools. We had received the plans for the Tahiti Ketch, the boat we were planning to build at the time, and to keep the sailing dream alive among the gophers and the grain elevators we decided to start the lofting process on our Sundays off.

During the homestead era the little farm community of Floweree had supported a blacksmith's shop, a school, a store with a gas pump, a post office, a rail depot, a hotel and a church. But sixty years of harsh Montana weather had taken its toll on the population and on the buildings. Still the church stood four square and upright, like the Methodist circuit rider, Brother Van, who had preached there. The siding was weathered and warped and all the windows were broken out. The plaster continued to fall from the high ceiling like an intermittent hail storm, a process that had been going on for forty years. The old pump organ was no longer there, but careful listening on a quiet Sunday morning would reveal the faint strains of *The Old Rugged Cross.*

The old building had served as a venue for countless church services, potlucks and square dances and in my teenage years it had been our winter basketball court. That summer was undoubtedly the first time it had been used as a lofting floor for a sailboat. It was the only large wooden floor in the area that we could drive nails into. We tacked down our sheets of plywood and started the lofting process. To avoid being irreverent, I refrained from blasphemy, tried to maintain humble thoughts and, of course, spent most of my time on bended knee. The summer flew by, and when the snow started drifting onto the floor, we knew it was time to return to Belize.

Now we had fourteen sheets of plywood tacked to the floor of the new boat shed and had been lofting in earnest. I had spent ninety hours, so far, and thought this phase of the project was almost finished when I came to an impasse; there was a lump in one of the horizontal waterlines. If I faired it into a smooth curve, the lump just appeared somewhere else, like a fat lady in Spandex. I could spread the lump out, but it was still there, less pronounced but broader. I would have challenges enough without starting with uneven molds.

Our son Scott, upon seeing me sitting on a pig-tail bucket and staring at the floor like a tropical version of "The Thinker," came up with his usual greeting, "How's it goin'?" He was a nice-looking eighteen-year-old with light brown hair, a tall, slender build and a good sense of humor. "Experimenting with a little psychokinesis are you?"

I explained my dilemma, and put a batten in place to demonstrate the lump. He stared at it awhile and then sighted from each end. "It would look pretty good if you could bring it out a little here at station nine." The lofting was divided into stations every three feet from bow to stern.

"Okay, I'll try it but it will change the body plan there." It took several sets of lines to define any point in three dimensions and a change in one line caused a change in its partners. I moved the batten out a quarter of an inch which took the lump away nicely. Surprisingly the body plans at stations 9 and 8 looked even better than they had before. Resolution! That's all you could call it.

The lofting had been a fascinating and rewarding process in that way. There was a lot of trial and error, but when it was right it felt perfect, not just better—like finding the right piece for a puzzle or getting the right shape for a bowl. I knew there must be a rational explanation, but it was too complex to fully understand, and frankly, I didn't feel the need to. I hoped all the building steps would prove to be as satisfying as this one had.

I would waste no time before starting on the molds. These were the full-sized bread slices that would determine the shape of the hull—wide molds in the middle of the boat narrowing toward the ends. They were made strong with plenty of bracing but with unfinished lumber since they would serve only to give the proper shape to the hull and would not be a permanent part of the finished boat.

Scott came running out in mid-afternoon as if wasps were chasing him. He had been in the house listening to the radio. "Dad, they just gave the chalice to the Pope. We're famous!" It was one of those unforgettable moments in life. It is not always possible at the time to recognize the significance of an honor that has been bestowed upon us, and perhaps I hadn't fully appreciated the tribute I had received by being chosen to make this gift. But that honor was totally overshadowed by this expression of respect from my teen-aged son. Sons are known to spend lifetimes seeking approval from their fathers and can become unhinged when that approval is withheld. What is usually learned too late is that a father needs his son's recognition, too. I felt I had just received his blessing.

5

~~~

April-June 1983

CHASING THE RABBET

With the lofting phase complete and temporary molds built, it was time to actually start on the permanent parts of the boat. It was an exciting moment, but the feeling was tempered by the fact that the first structural member of our wooden boat was ferrocement. I kept glancing toward the trail entrance to make sure no wooden boat purist would arrive and catch me in the act.

Our sailing experiences had shown that occasional groundings were inevitable in Belize's reef-strewn waters, resulting in the loss of the protective copper paint. We decided to make the lowest timber on the boat, the sacrificial shoe, out of concrete. Typically it was a wooden timber that needed to be replaced every few years due to damage from the wood-boring toredo worms. We hoped the concrete would last indefinitely and its extra weight would reduce the amount of internal ballast required.

A wooden mold, four inches deep, six inches wide and twenty-four feet long, was built with wooden plugs at intervals to form holes in the casting for keel bolts. Care was taken so the reinforcing rod was completely imbedded, and an extra rich mix was used to make this concrete beam waterproof. It is extremely unlikely Pete designed the boat for a concrete shoe, still, he probably didn't expect this boat to be used in tropical waters and as a builder himself, he would likely have appreciated this commonsense approach.

I suppose everyone experiences the maximum satisfaction if they feel their creation is an original, but I planned to limit my innovations to the building process and would try to duplicate Pete's hull shape as closely as possible. I had seen the performance of a fine boat compromised by modifications introduced by the builder, and I didn't want to make the same mistake.

Some years before, friends had arrived on their maiden voyage of the *Here and Now*. Tony and Debra had discovered the skeleton of a 32-foot sloop, its ribs baking on the banks of Haulover Creek in Belize City. It was the second of an intended series of "Belizean Cutters". An American entrepreneur had recognized the exceptional skills of Simeon Young, one of the best Belizean boat builders of the time, and decided to capitalize. For unknown reasons, the production run stopped after number one was completed and number two was only started. The entrepreneur probably returned home with a small fortune, small at least, compared to the one he had arrived with. Belize is like that.

Tony and Debra had bought the frame and finished the boat themselves over a several-year period. Scott and I were invited for a two-day, shakedown cruise to the nearby cays. We were along as friends and sailing enthusiasts but also to provide "local knowledge." The trip did not go smoothly.

From Orange Point our destination was West Snake Cay, 18 miles to the northeast. The morning land breeze left us becalmed halfway, and we had drifted aground onto the shallow banks east of Moho Cay. After setting an anchor out in deeper water and kedging ourselves off, we reached our destination in the evening and spent a pleasant night in an idyllic setting of crystal-clear water, palm trees and white sand. Early the next morning we set out on our return trip to Orange Point against a light southwesterly breeze. I assured Tony that it would back around during the morning hours into a fair northeasterly.

We soon discovered something very disturbing about the new boat—it would not sail to windward. Though no sailboat can go directly into the wind, it is expected to sail 60 degrees or closer to the direction the wind is coming from. Tacking back and forth, like climbing a zigzag stairway, will eventually bring it to its upwind destination. We sailed back and forth a lot of miles that sunny afternoon but made very little progress toward Orange Point. To make matters worse, the wind had picked up to 15 knots and remained right on the nose. At dusk the storm clouds moved in from the north and the rain began.

It was my watch, and it was indeed a dark and stormy night. My plastic poncho hadn't kept the rain out and I was soaked through. I envied Scott, Tony and Debra in their warm, dry bunks below. Sometime in those wee, wet hours I glanced astern to see a small red light, soon lost in the rain. In a few minutes it reappeared, this time much closer and with a green partner. Its distance above the sea told me I was looking at the bow lights of a large and close vessel that was heading directly for us. I could feel the throb of big diesels, and the bow wave sounded like a fast-moving stream. I yelled down to Tony for a flashlight, which he trained on our sails in an effort to avoid being run down. A moment later we were blinded by a huge search light. The impact never came, and after a minute the light went off. By the time my vision returned, the green light had gone and the red light was fading into the mist.

Dawn revealed the nearby shoreline of Guatemala and the very distant Saddleback Hill near Punta Gorda, where we expected to be. A few miles to the west, a British frigate (undoubtedly our night time visitor) cruised—apparently protecting Belize against an invasion force of sailboats. Slowly the wind backed around to the south and we were able to point directly to Orange Point. It was a tired and rather subdued crew that anchored up that evening. It had been an educational trip for all of us. I decided not to go into weather forecasting or into piloting as a profession. It was clear that four sailors who know a little don't add up to one sailor who knows a lot. But the most pertinent lesson was related to boat design.

Preferring the look of a counter stern, Tony had extended his boat by three feet. He had the eye of an artist and she turned out to be a real beauty. But the added weight aft brought the bow up, changing her underwater profile, and she had lost the balance necessary for sailing to windward. Adding weight to the bow would help but she probably would never sail as well as she would have without the alteration.

We had a fair collection of books on boatbuilding and with several years of observation had a good idea of how Belizean boats were put together plus the kind of sailing conditions we could expect in Belizean waters. I had watched John Baldwin, Punta Gorda's own boat builder, construct two boats, one of which we eventually bought. "Amigo" lived on Front Street, only a hundred yards from the sea. His clapboard house was unpainted, but his lady, Miss Lois, kept the yard in a riot of lovely tropical blossoms. A grassy lot nearby was vacant, except for a scattering of coconut and mango trees that provided just enough shade for his boatbuilding site.

He had ordered from the local mill, enough one-inch lumber for the planking and decking of the twenty-seven-foot fishing smack he was building on contract and enough extra for a twenty-two-footer for himself. His rib and deck beam stock were 2 X 4s; he used 4 X 4s for his keels and some wide four-inch flitches (raw-edged slabs) for deadwood. Along with the sawn lumber was an assortment of small branches that would be hewn down for the knees and the curved stems. Right away he put the planking stock to soak in salt water so it would leach the sap out and help stabilize the wood.

Boards nailed to a couple of tree trunks and a horizontal plank served as a work bench. His tools, all hand, included a pair of saws, a hammer, brace and bits, chisels, a gouge, a plane and a few clamps. Amigo was a trim Kriol man in his 60s who had built boats off and on his whole life. The plans he worked from were stored in his brain from all those years of experience. He seemed to know exactly what he wanted to do and how to go about getting it done. He was skilled at using his tools and his construction techniques were simple, fast and appropriate for the end function—producing quickly and economically an easily-repaired boat for use in protected waters.

Of particular interest to me was his technique of beveling the top corners of the keel to make a landing for the lowest row of planks. It was much easier than cutting a full length notch (rabbet) in the keel as my books called for, but seemed weaker and harder to caulk. Amigo explained that if you notched in the frames and planking, the keel would be hard to replace. It was plenty strong this way and when it leaked too much you just needed to haul it out and recaulk it. Though he never appeared to be in a hurry, at the end of nine months both boats were completed, moved on rollers to the seaside with rum power (hand labor) and launched.

Amigo and Miss Lois christened their little sloop, *Morning Star,* and sailed her to and from their home in the cays for several years before they moved back to town. Amigo was right all around. After three years, he had hauled her out on the beach at his cay where he hewed a timber out of a white mangrove tree and replaced the keel in a few days. After we bought her, when she leaked too badly, we hauled her out and re-caulked her—many times.

In the same way the best designs are related to their planned use, construction details must be customized for function, in our instance, how and where we would use the boat. We didn't plan to cross oceans but we wanted to build her strongly, just in case we decided to venture out into the Caribbean. So, with a few modifications, we used the stout construction plan for the ocean-going Tahiti Ketch and we employed Skene's naval architect rules to determine frame and centerline scantlings (dimensions). In spite of the extra effort, the garboard plank and frame ends would be notched into the keel, making the boat much stronger and easier to keep water tight. A leaking boat in mid-Caribbean was a disturbing prospect.

Along with the shapes of the molds, the loft floor showed the outline for the backbone assembly. In addition to the ferrocement shoe, it would be made up of seven or eight large pieces of wood. By developing our own construction plan, we had a lot of flexibility in how we put them together. This freedom was soon applied in fitting the keel timber to the stem and stern posts. If I squared the ends for traditional butt joints, the timber would be six inches too short. In a moment of panic, I considered the magnitude of the problems that would result in trying to shorten the boat by a half foot. After getting myself together I realized that if I butted the keel against the stern post, rather than vice versa, I would have almost an inch to spare. I then made a miter joint to join the wooden inner shoe to the stern post. It was more complex but the end grain of the three timbers, always vulnerable to rot and ship worms, would be protected. It was the first of many experiences on the project where, with careful planning and the element Tina called magic, there would be just enough material, and the end result was better than expected.

The keel timber was the most important structural member on the boat and what a marvel it was. When I had originally gathered the framing lumber, Melvin's men had looked for a pine log specifically for this purpose and after several weeks had found it. I had ridden the bulldozer into the bush a few miles to look at it. A tall pine had blown down some unknown years before. The sapwood had all rotted away leaving only the rich resinous heart. The men called it lighter pine, not because of its weight (it wouldn't have floated), but because even a splinter would hold a flame like a torch. Leaving it as long as possible, Jose had bucked it up, we had skidded it out and rough cut it on the mill.

Fashioning the backbone assembly was like making pieces for a giant puzzle from massive blocks of wood and then bolting them all together. The rough-sawn Santa Maria timbers were seven inches in thickness, fourteen in width and from five to eight feet in length. The keel timber was almost twenty-six feet long, seven inches wide and ten inches deep. Straightening, flattening and shaping these large chunks were new experiences, and having no spare pieces, I worked slowly and carefully.

There were times when only hand tools would do the job and I had learned to use the axe and adz with a certain level of competence, but I didn't feel bound by tradition, and the chain saw, skill saw and planer were used whenever possible. Holes for the longest through-bolts were bored with a hand-turned ship's auger. Feeling the resistance of the bit was essential since breaking it off in a three-foot hole would have spelled disaster. Shorter holes were bored with an electric drill. Bolts were fabricated by cutting and threading galvanized rod that was bought locally in twenty-foot lengths.

Because of its constantly changing bevels, the rabbet had taken many hours to cut, using a bevel gauge, chisel, mallet and rabbet plane. One morning, in the middle of the several days I had spent on this step, I looked out to see *Sunalee* riding very low in the water. I bailed out nearly a hundred gallons, pushed in more caulking cotton from the outside into the garboard seam and went back to my rabbeting project with renewed purpose.

The old boat builders recommend stopping now and then to savor what has been accomplished, so one won't be overwhelmed by the prospect of how much lies ahead.

Standing upright before me was the result of months of work. The golden-yellow, freshly-planed, pine keel contrasted nicely with the red of the Santa Maria posts and knees and the purple of the bastard rosewood stem shoe. Running from the top of the stem, down and along the keel and on up to the stern was the continuous rabbet that would accept the plank edge. We had only begun, I realized, but it was a start and it was real. Visitors would now be able to recognize that it was a boat we were building, not an airplane or a chicken coop.

6

~~~

June - December 1983

SYNERGISM

"My goodness, she has a big arse!" I exclaimed as I helped Kirby put the transom frame into place.

"It's not polite to make comments on a lady's posterior when she doesn't have her planks on," he quipped.

Lofting the transom had been a challenge since it was raked 30 degrees to the sight line of the beholder. Kirby had commented at the time, "The transom is not actually seen as it is made, so to make it look right, I must fair lines that don't exist. How's that for a challenge? I don't know whether to consult a boatbuilding book or a philosophy text."

The station molds, ready and waiting, were set up on the backbone at three-foot intervals, and then ribbands, two-inch square strips, were fastened horizontally around them. We now had length, height and width that allowed me to truly visualize the shape of the boat evolving out here in the jungle. It was an exciting moment.

The next step was bending in the frames (ribs), the upright timbers that would define her shape much as our ribs determine ours. Local boat builders would have sawn the frames to shape. Having read that steamed ribs make for a more resilient hull with fewer fastenings needed, we decided to steam and bend them into the required curves. The lower ends of the frames would fit into the sockets Kirby had carved in the keel, 1¾ inch square, one every twelve inches on each side, sixty in all.

Pete Culler would have recommended white oak for framing because oak has long tube-like fibers that easily absorb steam and can be bent to nearly any shape. We hoped to find a tropical species that could be substituted.

We began our experimenting with Santa Maria. Its wavy grain ran off the sides of the sawn stock and it separated when bent. Mahogany's grain is straight and it is very stable but it would not do well with our galvanized fastenings.

We had on hand a few pieces of cabbage bark, a straight-grained, dense and durable secondary wood. In our experiments we found that it would bend fairly easily but cracked after cooling. The steaming process was apparently drying it out and making it brittle. I decided to try some tamale technology (Belizean tamales are wrapped in leaves before cooking). I packaged each piece of frame stock in plastic sheeting and after a few hours of steaming it became fairly flexible and did not break or splinter when cool. We headed up the road for more cabbage bark.

On the way to the mill we noticed several piles of freshly-cut rosewood logs. We depended on rosewood for our craft business, and though we had good connections for getting off-spec logs and branches, we always had our eyes open. We stopped in at the government forest station. Sammy, the chief officer, said the international market for rosewood had just shot up, and everyone and their brother wanted to cut it. All the big pines and most of the mahogany were gone—now rosewood? "Is there a program for replanting?" I asked.

He shrugged, "There probably is, but it has never been implemented—not enough staff or money. Since independence each department is supposed to be self-supporting. We make our income from licenses and royalties when trees are cut, not when they are left standing."

When Belize became self-governing in 1964, it inherited colonial institutions which were based on exploitation, not conservation. It was all the little country could do to keep functioning without thinking of changing philosophy. We began to wonder what we would do once the forests were gone. When we came to British Honduras we found what we thought was a sustainable way of life, one that depended on the forest cycles. We felt our rosewood cottage industry fit right in. It took very few logs to provide us a living, it was renewable and we had replanted far more trees than we had used.

It was obvious that, to the government, trees were only a commodity. It was also clear that, in general, those involved in the timbering business were not thinking about long term sustainability. Their concessions to cut on government lands were of short duration, and there was no incentive to plant when it was likely someone else would reap the benefits.

A month later, India, the world's largest rosewood trader at that time, started exporting wood again, and the international market plummeted overnight. The piles of rosewood were never picked up, and they continued to bake in the hot sun, cracking and rotting. Soon they were good for nothing but firewood. Our emotions were in turmoil. Knowing the importance of trees in the cycles of the Earth, this seemed like outright vandalism, wanton destruction of the forest. It was hard to not give in to despair. We vowed we would protect the little forest at Orange Point.

My tamale method kept the frames from becoming brittle but still they broke where the curves were sharpest. Kirby ripped the stock down the middle. We bent in one half, let it cool and bent in the other half on top. When both were cool we separated the two S-shaped pieces and smeared the joining surface with a thick layer of bedding compound, then screwed them tightly together.

We found much of the boat work required two sets of hands, with one pair just as important as the other. For the framing job Kirby cut the strips. I operated the steam box, kept the wood fire going, wrapped and loaded the frame stock and made the decision as to when the pieces were ready to bend. I passed the hot pieces up to Kirby. From the inside he bent and walked them out against the ribbands. I lined them up in the sockets and clamped them in place. Finally, after our initial experiments and many long days of straining work, we had a forest of frame heads reaching for the roof of the boat shed.

A reasonable degree of productivity was essential to ever finish a project this big, and both of us learned a lot about personal work patterns. Kirby focused on the how-to-do-it aspects of the project aided by his common sense and well-developed reasoning powers. As important as figuring out the tasks that needed to be done was determining the sequence for the doing. He possessed skill with the tools and was adept at improvising for the ones he didn't have. He lathed each morning to keep our craft business going, and by the time he finished he had his boat work planned for the day.

He liked to start the day with some simple task to warm up on, like boring the holes for fastenings. He discovered it was best to put down his tools if a visitor came to talk (a frequent event). According to him, his brain only had one channel and trying to work and talk at the same time was counterproductive because of the mistakes he was likely to make.

He found he reasoned more clearly in the early part of the day. No matter how relaxed he felt, important decisions, like whether or not a plank would need steaming, were not to be made in the evening of a hard day. Additionally, he discovered that his mind could solve problems subliminally if he went over the details and let them ferment for a while. The answers often arrived in the wee hours. Expecting immediate results by worrying a problem like a dog with a bone was far less productive.

We did the planning together and shared our accomplishments, but it took time and struggle to work out a rhythm so we weren't in each other's way. Our experience in re-building our little sloop, *Sunalee*, had been a lesson we had to perfect on this job. Still, short of rest, short of money, short of patience, our marriage of twenty-plus years was often tested in ways it had not yet been.

"If you had just told me I wouldn't have smeared pine tar all over that surface—I thought you were through."

"Where's my chisel? It doesn't go in that box. It belongs on the shelf!"

"Do you have to sand that right now? I really don't want sawdust all over this surface I'm ready to goop."

"You shouldn't have plugged those screw holes yet—I have to take that plank off one more time."

With time, despite these irritations, we became more and more aware of the synergy in our working relationship. I drew on the information that had pooled somewhere in my brain from reading a broad variety of material we had gathered over the years. A great deal of those bits and pieces came from *WoodenBoat Magazine* and the *Mariner's Catalogs*. My Uncle Jim had given us his boatbuilding library, and I augmented it by sending for any literature I thought would benefit us.

Sailors often wrote about maintaining their vessels and the gear necessary to sail them. This information gave me a long-term perspective on the use of our vessel. Pete Culler himself had many ideas about the necessary care of wooden craft, what worked and what didn't. He believed in the old ways and that philosophy meshed well with the basic materials we had to work with; I did my best to incorporate these ideas into the construction process. I discovered I have an uncanny ability to find the right book for providing answers to immediate and important questions—as if my hand is being directed to them. This turned out to be an important skill since books played such a large role in the construction process. Kirby became appreciative of my larger perspective and came to depend on my input.

As well as working in the shop, I kept the household running. Over the sink I often pondered the outcome of putting all our resources into building this boat and how we would be able to maintain her. I tried to imagine what living aboard would be like and whether we would embrace it. But more importantly, I wondered how much this experience was changing us and if we would we want a life afloat. This project was turning out to be as much about self-discovery as about sailboats.

Thirty-two large, trapezoidal chunks of heavy Caribbean pine were shaped into athwart ship floor timbers, one for each pair of frames. They were notched over the keel and fastened to it with long, galvanized drift bolts. The ends were cut to the shape of the frame and bolted to it with carriage bolts. It took time and patience to bevel and carve these timbers, but Kirby said he felt like a real boat builder when he was using the adz.

These timbers are critical in bonding the lower part of the boat together, much as our love holds our relationship together when it is under stress. And certainly the hard work and long hours introduced plenty of that; surprisingly we felt our bond to each other growing stronger under those conditions.

CHANCE ALONG

The late evening sun flooded the shed as we climbed between the ribs to sit on the new floors. I loved this time of reflection—savoring what we had accomplished and preparing to meet the next day's challenges. Tensions fell away as we sat and enjoyed the sight of her coming together. Taking time to dream, to reassess and to gain perspective was as important as the work itself.

It was during these intervals we became aware that together we were creating something special—much more than just a composition of boards and nails. In these moments of quiet we could feel the gathering energy—vibrations of an existence ready to burst forth.

7

~~~

February-December 1984

IN TOUCH WITH MY HANDS

In Punta Gorda, Carroll's yard, where Amigo had built the two smacks, was a popular place for boat work. The water was deep enough close to shore for Julio to haul up his cargo boat, *Rebecca,* for plank replacement and caulking. A thirty-foot log, five feet in diameter, had been roughed out where it was felled in the bush and floated here for finishing. Now Herbert, one of the local dory builders, had pulled it up and was working on it in the shade of a mango tree.

When there was boat work being done in the area, I usually found time to watch—taking the opportunity to learn some new techniques. Herbert was considered a master with the adz and I hoped some of his skills would rub off on me if I watched closely enough. I had used the tool to rough out the flat faces of the centerline timbers but trimming the concave ends of the floors had shown my lack of finesse.

Herbert sat on a small stool inside the roughed-out log taking short, deft strokes across the grain. The angle at which the cutting edge met the wood and the force applied were critical. I paid a lot of attention to his hands, now well separated to get better control—those scarred and gnarly, yet perfectly coordinated old hands. The rhythmic chip, chip, chip had a hypnotic effect on me in the warm afternoon breeze.

Man, as an animal, has a lot of deficiencies; he can't fly, swims poorly, is slow at climbing trees and doesn't run very fast. His senses of sight, smell and hearing are nothing to brag about either, but he has exceptional skills at doing things with his hands, foremost among them is the making and using of tools. Individual skills vary, but everybody has them—some are good with a mandolin and others with a machete, some wield a pen and others a plane. Skills are an essential part of the creativity kit we were each born with. Kids naturally play trucks, build sand castles, make sling shots, kites and doll houses, bake mud pies and cuddle babies. Life is all about discovering which skills we have and learning how to employ them to put form to our creative urges.

The chipping stopped and I roused from my contemplation. I passed Herbert my bag of mangos and took a couple for myself. "The adz is a dangerous tool," Herbert declared between slurps, and he showed me the scar on his shin to prove his point. He said if I valued my *cojones* (manhood) I would position myself so the top of the cutting stroke was never above the waist. As I stood up to go, leaving him the remainder of the fruit, he stated, "I got my cigarettes," he held up all three, "and now I got my hairy mangos!" That small bounty and the few swallows of rum left in his pint made his day. We shared mango smiles—ocher-stained mouths with a few strings still caught between our teeth—and I started toward home. I envied Herbert's skill with the adz but also his ability to get such joy from each day's simple pleasures, something that often eludes those of us who are burdened with the need to follow a plan.

So far, planning was all the planking process had consisted of. Several years before, I had bought enough pine stock to sheathe the hull, but with very little to spare. Now most of the big pine trees were gone from the forest, and even if I could find wide, heartwood lumber, it would be unseasoned and subject to further shrinkage. To avoid waste, each piece from my stock had been numbered, measured and carefully evaluated for its length, width-of-heart and its shape. After calculating the area to be covered, I made up a plan for the dimensions of each of the nearly one hundred pieces that would be used to sheathe the hull. Full-length planks were not available and the joints, where shorter pieces came together, had to be carefully spaced so a weakness in the hull would not be introduced. I planned it so butts in adjacent planks were separated by at least three feet. I am sure Amigo could have planked the whole boat in the period of time it took me to get ready.

Determining the tool requirements for this type of boatbuilding began the day the plans arrived and we started collecting tools during our summer in Montana. Tina's dad had given us a good set of basic do-it-yourselfers and I added a table saw from a garage sale, kits to make a band saw and a lathe, a big drill from Sears and an adz from a specialty tool supply. My Uncle Walt, a John Deere dealer, had donated a new 1800-watt generator since we were off the grid at Orange Point. Most of the required tools were common to home craftsmen and were easily obtained, but ships' augers were unheard of in the local hardware stores and I had to admit that Montana was a strange place to be looking for them. They are unique—not only in their length, but in a tip design that allows them to cut long, straight holes through wood with a contrary grain. I knew that boring for the long centerline bolts would be a challenge even with the proper tools so I kept looking.

Upon hearing of my quest, my brother suggested I look in Charlie's tool chest. The tools had been left to Russ when the old bachelor blacksmith died. Charlie had homesteaded in Montana in 1910 but his income came mainly from his skills as carpenter, farrier and blacksmith for the community. When I was young, I remember cranking the bellows on the forge while Charlie hammered out a hinge. He spit tobacco juice on it occasionally to judge its temperature or maybe to apply a special tempering process. At the bottom of that old steamer chest, I found exactly what I was looking for—a set of long, barefoot augers. Later when I bored the centerline timbers, I felt Charlie would have been glad to have them put to use. He may even have sent down a spiritual squirt of Copenhagen for lubrication to keep them cutting clean and true.

A week after my adz lesson Tina and I were taking turns on top of the stepladder. We had set it up fifty yards from the boat shed and used it to get a horizontal view of the uppermost row of planks, the sheer strake. "What do you think?" I asked. She has a critical eye when it comes to judging boats and the sheer is always the most noticeable line. The planks had an "S" curve when laid flat on the floor but when twisted into place gave the bow a pleasing upsweep.

She studied it again carefully, "It's not delicate like an Alden, but for this kind of boat it's perfect!" Each designer has his own idea of what makes a pretty boat and the sheerline can become his signature feature. Pete Culler was no exception. It was only after we had added a mock bowsprit, similar to what the finished boat would have, that we could see the perfection of his line. It gave us the confidence that we were on our way toward producing a lovely boat.

Though each plank was unique in shape, a pattern in the process developed. A ribband, the temporary strap that held the frames in place, was removed to make space for the new plank. The frames and floor timbers were checked for fairness so the planks would lay flat against them. In the lower aft section the frame curves were concave and I trued them up with the adz and a rocker-bottomed, rosewood plane made specifically for this purpose.

A spiling batten, a thin board roughly the shape of the plank, was clamped in place and marked every foot. The edge of the new plank was found by transferring these marks to the plank stock. Its width was predetermined by its position fore and aft in the hull. The roughed-out plank was shaped on the inside face so it would lie tightly against the curved frame. Temporary positioning showed where the gaps existed between the new plank and the one already fastened in place. The plank was unclamped and these gaps were removed by planing the edge at the proper bevel.

Several trials were usually necessary before an acceptable fit was accomplished. I avoided much of the subjectivity in deciding when the fit was close enough by establishing the thickness of a hacksaw blade, approximately a thirty-second of an inch, as the maximum allowable gap. The outer 2/3 of the plank's edge was beveled slightly to allow for later caulking and finally a duplicate, or to be more accurate, a mirror image of the plank was prepared for the other side. Hot-dipped, galvanized screws and boat nails were soaked in Tina's special brew of pine tar and turpentine and used to fasten the planks to the frames and butt blocks.

I spent an average of eight hours in planing, measuring, shaping and fastening each plank. My fits became better as I went along, and I became a little faster. I started at the sheer and worked my way down, stopping just below the turn of the bilge (bulge) where the planks had the least twist and curve. Then I moved to the lowest plank (garboard) and started working my way back up. This thick and wide plank was a challenge due to its extreme twist. As with the other planks, Tina sealed the ends and bedded the butt block before helping me clamp and fasten this brute into place. We were just standing back congratulating ourselves for finally getting the first garboard in position, when, with the sound of a pistol shot, it split. With no spare lumber left, the next pieces were wrapped in burlap and steamed prior to installation. I also discovered that stress in the plank and in the builder could be reduced by carving in some of the twist.

After eleven-hundred hours spread out over eleven months, we finished the job. Tina used a twister on one end and I tapped the "shutter" plank into the only remaining gap on the hull. It was just snug enough to stay in place while I bored for the fastenings. It was a moment of celebration—she was a real boat now and we had proved ourselves to be competent builders, not fast, but competent. By toasting the accomplishment with rosewood goblets full of local wine, we introduced a ritual for the end of each major step of the process.

And then there was the mystical element. When we first bought lumber, seven years before, I had set aside forty, thick, wide and tight-grained pine boards to use below the waterline. When we finished, there was only one board left—the one I had broken when I hadn't steamed it sufficiently. There had been just enough—no more. It was amazing.

Even though our estimates of completion time kept moving away like the end of a rainbow, the work continued to be satisfying. Each morning I could physically see the evidence of what had been accomplished the day before. In this regard I counted myself among the fortunate. I began to understand why it is said that few endeavors require the variety of skills that boatbuilding does; at the same time, few are as rewarding.

8

~~~

February 1985

IT'S ABOUT TIME

It is 2:00am when I roll over to see Kirby's eyes wide open in the moonlight.

"Can't sleep?"

"I had a dream that started me thinking about fitting the sheer clamp. I have some ideas I better write down." He lifts the mosquito net and is gone.

I remain in bed assessing our situation.

Kirby claims that in order to complete any large project one must convince himself that he is nearly done, even if reality says otherwise. He had overlooked reality when we started building, first with his estimate of building costs and most of all with his estimated launch date.

Time is a very subjective concept and is undoubtedly influenced by one's culture. Ramón had moved his family into town from the Maya village of Pueblo Viejo. Coming into the Kriol and Garifuna culture had been a hard transition (almost as radical as our own had been), but he wanted his children to have a chance to go to high school, and Punta Gorda had the only one in the district. We passed by their little thatched house, full of kids and laughter, on our way to town. We had become friends, partly because we shared the status of outsiders. Soon after we laid the keel, Ramón had asked how long it would take to build the boat.

"Probably three years," Kirby said.

"But what if you de dead?"

Dying while still in our early 40s wasn't an issue that we had considered. Though he was ten years younger, the chance of his dying seemed to preclude Ramón from starting such a long term project. Still, while our minds were dealing with future problems, his was free to enjoy each day to the fullest.

One day he and his brother brought out a small stone artifact and asked Kirby how he thought the ancient Maya bored the hole in it. Even Kirby, who admonishes himself for always taking people too literally, recognized the real question as, "Do you want to buy this stone?" As he told it, he gave the two Mayas a ten minute monologue on how important cultural heritage is and that the artifact belonged to the whole Maya nation; it was indeed a part of their patrimony and should never be sold, but should be donated to a museum. Ramón responded, "But Mr. Kirby, what if you just want to go drink rum?"

Yes, indeed. What if you just want to build a boat?

We tried to give the majority of our daily hours to that task. Some days we managed and some days we didn't, but it was always uppermost in our minds despite the other distractions. The process continued at a subliminal level causing a constant drain on our energy as well as a distraction from the other demanding parts of our lives. Still, I knew we had gone too far to ever think of stopping. But the rub seemed to be time.

In wanting to live on the water we may have been seeking simplicity, but we were finding there was nothing simple about the boatbuilding itself, nor in trying to finance it. We started with enough lumber to complete the hull and planking. We were aware that this was only a small portion of the cost of the finished boat, and we planned to sell *Sunalee* and the bus to finance some of the pricier pieces of equipment. For the day to day costs of the construction such as fuel, saw blades and sand paper we counted on earnings from our craft business. We were pushing it as hard as we could.

We had worked out much of the inefficiency in operating KirbyKraft by no longer delivering every order in person. Agreements had been made with several gift shops in the tourist centers of Belize City and Ambergris Cay under which we filled their orders and sent them up by air; they received the items and mailed us a check—usually. We also took orders from British army officers, missionary groups and individuals who lived in the Punta Gorda area, thus doing a lot of custom work. For a cottage industry it was really quite successful, but neither Kirby nor I inherited the capitalistic skill of hiring the work done, so every dollar we earned represented time we personally spent in the shop. Boat materials required money, which required shop time—time that couldn't be spent on boatbuilding. It was a balancing act that started with lofting and would not end before the launch.

Visitors demanded a great deal of our time. We had made our business reputation by offering uniquely personalized items and for the buyer that often included meeting and visiting with the craftsman. Kirby lathed from three to six hours a day depending on what orders we had, but he always lathed. When all of our orders were filled and he was working on speculation, more hours were spent on the boatbuilding. When the structure began to resemble a boat, people started walking out or arriving by skiff to see it. We never knew if they were coming to buy rosewood or just look at the boat. No matter how busy we were we gave them our time in hopes we would sell them a bowl, and because we had an innate politeness that wouldn't let us turn them away.

Our days didn't end when the sun went down. Planning was an essential part of this creative process, and much of it was done when it was too dark to work in the shop. Kirby was very thorough in the journal he kept. He sometimes made full-sized drawings showing how he would fit various pieces together, where the fastenings would go, and what kind and size were needed. We had to make financial and transportation arrangements well in advance. Only rarely were we held up waiting for something we didn't have.

This process was our way of learning—taking what we'd observed and read about and putting it into a plan of action. It was time consuming but undoubtedly made the difference between success and failure, and in the long run it shortened the actual hands-on building time. Because Kirby had already done the steps in his mind there was very little question about how to proceed.

The maintenance of our homestead had been whittled down to a daily once-over to keep the termites from eating the buildings and the vines from choking off the fruit trees. When the house roof began to leak, we opted to replace the thatch with tarpaper over the plywood from the lofting floor—an expedient way to keep the bed dry. We had given up all the animals except the dogs and parrots when the children left home. Still we had to keep the engines running: the generator, the gas motor on the planer, the ancient mower and my precious, old, Hoover washing machine.

I kept up with *Sunalee's* maintenance and only required Kirby's help when she threatened to sink. I enjoyed the work and had a real affection for this feisty little craft; she had given us some exciting and wonderful trips. The time spent maintaining her was my way of staying connected with the water world and my dream of living on the sea.

I crawl out of the net—the small room is bright with moonlight through its many windows. Walking out onto the little porch overlooking the sea, I can hear an occasional fish flop on the surface of the water. Listening to the night's music, I am sure I hear a manatee breathe. Surveying my small natural kingdom, I too, take a deep breath.

Still, I feel a disturbing restlessness. Perhaps it is only the recognition that our timeline is totally unrealistic. Every phase of this building project has included many, many steps, most of which are not described in the boatbuilding books. Each has taken two or three times as long as we predicted. We are two years into this project and, at the most, are halfway. Yet, we can't squeeze another hour into our work day.

Kirby is constantly "fighting fires" to balance the income with the outgo and find enough time for all the work. It is clear that he really enjoys the project, has a gift for visualizing the finished product and the skill and concentration to interweave the complex steps. He is in his element as a craftsman—building a boat, the ultimate challenge.

The vessel, in many ways, is becoming an extension of his self. Watching him pour his essence into this effort wills me to give it all I have, too. But the water beckons to me;

my dreams are of sailing and I feel opportunity slipping by. Since it is the immediate hands–on experience that absorbs him, time is less of a factor. This difference creates tension for he is content and I am not. Most of the time he is too preoccupied to be aware of my emotional ups and downs; a couple of times I have been so discouraged I dissolved into a puddle of tears.

As if an ordained test of my fidelity, it was just such a time when Mark arrived for a visit. He had completed his huge trimaran and was on his shake-down cruise from the Rio Dulce to Punta Gorda. Though our contacts had been infrequent, we kept in touch through mutual friends regarding our boatbuilding projects.

He would soon leave for Panama and the Pacific. His partner had refused to go with him. He was looking for crew and, sensing my discouragement, he asked me, out of Kirby's hearing, to sign on. Though the boat was big, it was simply rigged and he thought the two of us could handle it. I weighed the possibilities all through the night. When Mark appeared the next morning he looked at me inquiringly. I gently shook my head.

After he was gone, Kirby, as if his sensory alarm had gone off, agreed to a few days away on *Sunalee* and we left the next morning. When I told him about Mark's offer, he asked if I was tempted. "Yes a bit, but only for the sailing. Still, it is nice to know that I am desirable, at least as crew. Don't worry—I'm committed to making our dream come true, however long it takes, but most of all I'm committed to you."

The sea, wind in the sails, lovely sunrises and sunsets and a lot of attention from my lover provided a spiritual renewal. I returned revived and ready to carry on, but most importantly, with restored patience.

Turning back into the room I take the steep flight of stairs down to the kitchen where I put a pot of water on to heat. As I sit down at the table where Kirby is writing by lamp light, he looks up at me with concern. "It is not just the clamp I have been thinking about. This thing on our west property line is worrying me. What does the government plan to do with 200 acres?"

Several days before, Ramón had stopped by, "I gone chop firewood, and I just stop to see the boat. I hear this morning from a Carib (Garifuna) lady; Government is taking all of Orange Point for a project. What you t'ink?"

"I no hear 'bout it," Kirby answered anxiously. The townspeople always knew when something was going on that would affect them. Most of them cooked on wood fires and the Orange Point area supplied much of what was used.

After exchanging news of each of our families he shouldered his axe, "I gone," and he started back toward home; he would pick up his load of wood on the way. He and his brother had visited only the week before so I knew he had come with a message rather than to see the boat.

At lunch we had discussed the rumor. Two other projects had been proposed for Orange Point during our tenure: a cement plant and the terminus of an oil pipeline originating in Guatemala. Being a point of land, the government assumed it to be a suitable site for a shipping port and had sent company engineers to the area. In both cases the projects were quickly scrapped after we showed them our depth charts. Even a medium-sized ship could get no closer than a mile due to the shallow water. But maybe this project didn't require a port. Individuals, even alien residents such as we were, could own land in Belize but the government, under special circumstances, could compensate the owner and take it back. We were frightened.

Shortly after lunch we were in the government office. Harry, the "Lands Man", was the son of a sawyer friend of ours. With only occasional references to his black ledger book, Harry could relate the past and present owners of any parcel in the district. He was a model public servant, official but not officious. "Government has acquired all the serviceman grants in a two-hundred acre block on Orange Point," he stated.

"What about ours?"

As he perused the papers in his hands we waited for the verdict.

"Yours was included in the initial plan," my heart sank, "but since you have built structures on it and are living there, they decided not to acquire it." Acquittal!

Kirby found his voice. "What do they plan to do with it?"

"That hasn't been made official yet."

On the way home we passed the huge tree that marked the corner of the servicemen's block. Most of the veterans who had been awarded these plots for their World War II service had never cleared their land, and it was a bountiful piece of hardwood forest. A dozen rosewood trees had been logged out of the area, and we had salvaged the branches to start our craft business. The left, right, left slashes in the bark of this old sapodilla certified that it had produced chicle for untold sticks of chewing gum; still it had remained aloof from decades of Man's folly. We prayed it would survive whatever was coming now.

Having kept our property, we felt magnanimous. Maybe this new project would do something for the community—a university campus under the lofty branches, for example. In a moment of overconfidence, we thought we could deal with it, no matter what the project was.

We are both quiet and thoughtful as we sip our warm milk. "I think we need a break for awhile . . . . Maybe it's time to sell *Sunalee*. We hardly use her. If we take a part of the money for the new sails, the rest will give us some financial relief. We would have to take a month away to sail north."

I let out my breath slowly. This is hard. I know he is right—we can no longer build the new dream without giving up some portion of the old. With tears near the surface, I nod.

With that in our minds we begin planning a sail to Cay Caulker and Ambergris Cay where we can get the best price for our little sloop. We will have to make the most of this sail for it will be our last until we launch the hull waiting out there in the moonlight.

9
~~~

January 1985

SUNALEE: SAIL AND SALE

It is dusk as *Sunalee* ghosts into New Haven Bay, twenty miles northeast of Orange Point. We have had the benefit of a southwest wind, a product of a cold front passing through Belize, and the blessing of a gorgeous sunset, the kind that is only possible with the high, cold-weather clouds. We pay our dues with a rolly night as the south swells sweep into the bay.

New Haven's shallow, protected harbor is a favorite stopover for small yachts while cruising the waters of Belize or making their way down the coast en route to the Rio Dulce. Anchored at the upper end of the bay are two vessels we know. One is *Adios,* Mike and Bonnie's 35' trimaran. Longtime live-aboards, they left the harbors of Florida for more secluded anchorages. A few dozen yards from them is the *Nube Blanca,* a 30' strip-planked sloop, owned and sailed by Jim and Gae. They brought her down from Houston after an extensive refit and are searching for their paradise.

Charlie, Bonny and their five children are the only residents in this remote, natural harbor. They arrived in 1978 aboard their classic New York 30, *Endymion.* Having pumped the bilges steadily during their sail from Florida, they decided to build a marine railway so they could haul out and caulk the old vessel. Now they make their living hauling and repairing boats.

Charlie has recruited the crews in the harbor to help bring *Sunalee* ashore. Power for pulling the cradle and boat up the inclined rails is supplied by a huge capstan scrounged from a derelict square-rigger. Horizontal poles are inserted in the circular cable drum and every able body in the vicinity, including the customer, is expected to push. Walking around the capstan, singing sea chanteys to the rhythm of the clinking mechanism is something to tell friends about and everyone except Charlie is glad to participate. Charlie always assigns himself the job of tailing the cable, keeping tension so it doesn't slip on the drum. He grumbles and grunts a lot to disguise the fact that others are doing the hard work

Sunalee comes up easily, looking tiny on the big cradle. Tina and I sand the bottom, recaulk and putty where needed then apply a coat of copper, antifouling paint to the

bottom and one of enamel to the topsides. Sand flies, paint fumes and sloping bunks encourage us to work quickly. The next day second coats of paint are applied. By seven in the evening, both elated and exhausted, we are in our bunks. After a stormy night, dawn finds us ready to launch. We spend the day cleaning and scrubbing the interior, readying ourselves for the next leg of our journey. In the evening we join the others for sundowners. I offer Charlie an ancient, 20-horsepower outboard in exchange for the haul-out and he accepts though he has no use for it either. He says if we can sell his Belizean sloop, the *Bonny C*, we can keep everything we get over $10,000. I am not excited since the old derelict will never bring anything close to that amount, but I agree to try.

In the morning the sun has just managed to break the suction from its watery bed when we round Punta Ycacos, a mile east of New Haven. For a few hundred yards we stay close to shore to avoid the off-lying shoals. Then a pod of about twenty dolphins, mostly mothers with youngsters, escorts us out into the main channel, their joy of life enveloping us like a fog. By motor sailing when the breeze is light and tacking when the wind finally comes, we reach Placencia harbor by evening. A nascent tourism industry is just beginning to replace fishing as a source of income and the next day we sell $175 in rosewood items to a new resort.

A fair wind carries us through the offshore cays and out to the reef the next day; the rare sighting of a sea turtle adds spice to a good day's sail. We enter the protected waters inside South Water Cay about four o'clock and think we have crossed some border—we are so used to living as a minority we are shocked by seeing hoards of white people ashore! The British army has an R&R camp providing adventure training; sailboards with sunburned soldiers dot the water like a channel of buoys. Sixty, environmental science students from the University of Maine, seem to cover every foot of the thin, white beach. We are acquainted with their leader who has another field station in Toledo and he asks if we have any craft items. The dinghy seat acts as our display table and we sell $200 worth of bowls and bangles. This is going to be a profitable trip even if we don't sell *Sunalee.*

We share the anchorage with a fishing smack from Sarteneja, a small Spanish-speaking village in northern Belize. Six men are living on this 27-foot boat for a trip that will last from ten days to two weeks. Its ice chest takes up most of the volume below and its little dories are used for diving during the day and some for bunks at night. We admire the simplicity and efficiency of their craft and they admire our little yacht for her looks. In spite of the differences in language, we share a feeling of camaraderie we hadn't felt with our compatriots on the nearby shore. We enjoy the lobster they give us in the evening, and we hope they enjoy the hot pancakes we take over to them in the morning. Soon both boats are underway.

For two more days, the wind, sometimes fair and sometimes not, takes us up the inside of the reef. Skimming along in the calm waters behind the Drowned Cays, *Sunalee* is at her best. We bear off toward Porto Stuck, a shortcut through a mangrove cay, and thread our way through its aquamarine channel. We are now in the shallow, turquoise waters of northern Belize and can see the bottom with exquisite clarity.

We anchor on the west side of Cay Caulker a little way from the town. We averaged 4 knots today and covered 40 miles. It has been physically taxing but at the same time invigorating. Hauling anchors, hoisting sails and always compensating for the movement of a small boat, make us feel fit. In addition, sailing seems to give us balance mentally and emotionally. We have worked together and have gotten satisfaction from performing at our best.

Swinging to the early-morning, southeast breeze, *Sunalee* dances gently in the protection of the cay. A good night's sleep has eased our exhaustion and left us in a contemplative mood as we think back over the last two years. We are proud of the boat we are building; its quality will exceed our expectations, but we are disappointed in our rate of progress. Nathaniel Hawthorne said, "Providence seldom vouchsafes to mortals more than that degree of encouragement which suffices to keep them at a reasonably full exertion of their powers." One of the goals of this trip has been to position ourselves where Providence could vouchsafe a little more encouragement upon us and we seem to have been successful. The joys, feelings of accomplishment and general emotional fulfillment resulting from making this trip have reaffirmed our choice to put all our resources and efforts into building a sailboat. We just have to stay with it.

Our coffee cups are empty and it is time to put on our selling hats. First we get fuel and water from the fishing cooperative then go visiting around, telling old friends that *Sunalee* is for sale. As I tack up posters in the restaurants and post office with all the particulars listed, I have second thoughts about letting her go, reinforced when a local resident tells me how pretty she was sailing in last evening.

Wooden houses with metal roofs rest on four to eight-foot pilings. Sprinkled out along the sandy lanes and along the windward edge of the cay, they fit the setting perfectly. Now and again we see a small concrete bungalow with a metal roof hidden amongst the coconut trees and flowering bushes. A few tour guides have opened shop below their homes. Restaurants abound, advertising both local and American food.

Until recently this fishing village's people were only attuned to the tides and currents, rain and sun, and the day's catch. Ten years ago the cay was discovered by young Americans who wanted a place to hang out in the winter, returning to the United States for seasonal jobs. They continued to come back, bringing younger adventurers with them. Cay Caulker has now become a place for laid-back tourists, divers, and aspiring sailors.

Sailing back and forth in front of the cay, anchoring where *Sunalee* will be seen to best advantage, we talk to a number of potential buyers; unfortunately, they have more enthusiasm than money. After catching up with friends, Kip and Patty, who are chartering their recently-purchased sloop, *Chinook,* we sail north to San Pedro Town on Ambergris Cay.

While the cay to the south is for the laid-back young, this rapidly-growing town is the Mecca of the well-to-do tourist. This once-picturesque, fishing village has turned into a world-famous, diving destination with all the attendant businesses. It has become a place of hurry and scurry both on land and on the sea. Although it is a bit like visiting another planet, it is the perfect place to parade *Sunalee.*

The rest of the week is spent sailing back and forth, relaxing and enjoying the compliments from passing boats, our "For Sale" sign conspicuous in the rigging. In the evenings and on rainy days we sell rosewood and visit with old friends. People are welcoming and flattering of our craftwork and our craft; we have a warm glow of satisfaction.

On our sail along the "drag" today, a young man hails us from a passing skiff, asking how much we want for our boat. After I answer, he says "I'm Jeff, I'll be in touch." We have followed up leads on several potential buyers and have shown the boat to many but so far we have no dollars in hand. It is late afternoon when he appears on Bowen's dock where we are hiding from the cold, north wind, in the lee of the big freight boat *Empress.* In the rain he quickly looks *Sunalee* over. "I will be back in the morning." I feel disappointed; he hasn't even let me show off her fine points or discuss her cutter rig and sailing abilities.

He is on the dock in the morning saying he will wire the money to our U.S. bank account. Later, when Tina's father calls to say the money has arrived, we make out a bill of sale, have my signature witnessed by a J.P., carry off our backpack of clothes and hand him the oars to the dinghy. It is that easy—but not easy at all.

We learned a lot about ourselves in rebuilding *Sunalee* and in sailing her for eight years; she played many roles for us: teacher, mentor, and magic carpet. But now, we remind ourselves, she is helping to finance our current building project—providing cash to support our creativity—and that makes parting with her a little easier. We take the morning water taxi into Belize City and catch the bus for the long ride back to Punta Gorda.

Feeling refreshed, we are eager to return to our project. With the sea in front and the forest on three sides, we recognize our good fortune to have such an environment to work in. Traditionally, artists, writers and musicians have gathered together in places like Greenwich Village, New Orleans, Paris, and Vienna, but it is the forest-sea environment that ferments *our* creative juices. We realize how dependent we are on this environment to sustain our efforts.

10

~~~

February 21, 1985

DEVESTATION

Dear Friend,
  Bull dozers came today—I am in shock!
Two D-9s with a huge logging chain between them, running in tandem, knocking down hundred-year-old forest like match sticks. I can hear the trees screaming. The animals are fleeing. It seems so totally brutal!
  The drivers say they will continue until they have thrown down two hundred acres behind our property. It seems there has been no forethought to save the timber; it will be cracked and bruised. It is very like a hurricane, yet such acts of Nature leave seeds for regeneration; the debris breaks down into humus that nurtures the rebuilding of this intricate web. The intent today is total destruction—after knocking it all down it will be burned. There is swagger in the men operating the machines—they appear drunk with power—human beings without conscience. I am so enraged!
  I imagine the Belizean Government is thinking of the promise of revenue. But good heavens, there are plenty of empty spaces in this country—how can they think of taking down more forest? And why aren't they at least salvaging what they can? I am wild with grief.
  I came here to get a broader perspective. I have been trying to learn to live in harmony with the earth systems by

CHISELS, CHIPS, AND CREATIVITY

seeing how other people live and solve their problems, how they relate to their environment. Up to now I have been struggling to achieve personal balance, but today when I heard the trees crying out, my struggle became universal. I know in my gut that this action is wrong. I cannot understand how people can destroy the source that gives them life.

I am so glad we have never considered cutting our forest; at least there will be some trees still standing that will give us a buffer. Looking at the destruction daily would surely drive us to total despair. I am also grateful that we are involved in this building project. Staying focused on it may save our sanity......

11

~~~

March 1985

ISMS WARRIOR

I hear the rumble of the engines, and I know they are on our bush road. There is a ball of heat in my gut; I feel it expand into my chest and then rise to my brain. I kill the generator, pull on my boots and hat, and grab the machete. I see it 50 yards away as it comes around the corner, its partner close behind. I don't slow up and neither do they. Five feet short of collision we both stop. I point with my machete and over the engine noise I shout, "Go back, this is private property!"

It is a ludicrous scene: on a narrow jungle trail, a middle-aged man in bush clothes and rubber boots is having a confrontation with a pair of British army tanks. The cannon muzzle is directly above his head. To carry out their orders, the soldiers must drive over this living obstacle. In the turret, behind and above the shielded driver, are two young soldiers with assault rifles. What does this infuriated man expect to do with his bush knife, bang on the armor in hopes of damaging their hearing? Yet neither his oral nor his body language can be misunderstood, and he is fully armed with passion. After a brief stare-down, the driver radios to his partner behind and the two monsters back up and disappear around the corner.

Arrogance! I can't stand any more of it without losing what remains of my sanity. It is too bad to take my anger out on a few blokes who are just following orders. They couldn't know this dirt track is our only way to bring in a lumber vehicle and churning it up in the rainy season will keep it impassible all year.

Arrogance, to a Belizean, is a sin, perhaps the worst sin of all, and those who practice it are punished in one way or another. This attitude seems to have rubbed off on me. I have had my issues with the Brits; many times they have used Orange Point for a site to practice their maneuvers. They don't ask—they just come and set up camp. If they don't cut the small coconut palms to use for camouflage and they pick up their trash and fill their fox holes when they leave, we get along. After all, if it wasn't for their presence in the 70's to deter Guatemala's claim to Belizean territory, I would probably be speaking Spanish.

The state of bliss attained during our sail to the northern cays was shattered the moment we saw the forest being destroyed. No, the core issue is not with the British army, it is with our new neighbor on the back property line—our own United States government, for we have found out that the site will be used for a Voice of America relay station.

We were aware when we came to Belize that this region has been the political playground for a century of U.S. administrations, but we had paid little attention to the details. In our naiveté we thought Belize, formerly a British colony, would be exempt. The recent invasion of Grenada, also a member of the Commonwealth, should have been a warning, but it is 1600 miles away. El Salvador, Nicaragua, Guatemala, Honduras and Panama are closer and have always been influenced by the big neighbor up north.

Talk about arrogance! Without any public consultation, they threw the forest down with bulldozers and will complete the destruction by burning it. This area has always supplied much of Punta Gorda with building materials, firewood and game meat. It has been an example of man coexisting with his fellow creatures—Nature in equilibrium where resources were harvested in a sustainable way. For us this forest was a reservoir of creative energy that nourished us. Now it is gone.

It was the last straw, this morning, when one of the engineers informed me they would need to clear a 30-foot swath of *our* property so they would have a buffer zone around *their* chain link fence. I believe myself to be mild-mannered, but at that moment a little violence seemed an attractive option. Yet, I know these people aren't making the decisions, they are just employees doing their jobs. I suspect if I go to President Reagan himself he will refer me to someone higher up—John Wayne perhaps. I am not thinking or acting rationally. Thank goodness we still have our land, and I have my boatbuilding and craftwork to wrap myself up in.

Carlos Castaneda believes the difference between an ordinary man and a warrior is that a warrior will take all aspects of life as a challenge while an ordinary man takes it either as a blessing or a curse. I can already see that getting along with my neighbor will be a challenge; it is hard to imagine I will ever see it as a blessing, but I will work hard to prevent it from being a curse.

Pounding on something with a hammer seemed like appropriate therapy to dispel my irritable mood, and I just happened to have a hull that needed caulking. I had fitted the planks together as closely as I could, leaving only an eighth inch "V" groove in each seam to accept the caulking. Since the first craft was floated, the primary goal for a boater has been to keep the water on the outside of the hull. A large variety of caulking materials have been used to this end: pounded tree bark, sawdust, flannel underwear and even pillows have been used successfully, depending on the circumstances. Oakum, coarse hemp fibers soaked in tar, would be used in a boat with larger seams but we used cotton, much like that found in an aspirin bottle, but in long strands. The narrowest seams required only part of a strand; in wider areas the strand was bunched up, *gagged,* to fill the gap.

I had a set of caulking irons that resembled dull, broad chisels; their tips, two inches wide, varied in thickness from a sixteenth to an eighth of an inch to suit the width and depth of the seam. I made my mallet from rosewood with a head heavy enough to maintain the momentum of my swing but not so heavy that it would wear my arm out. Every phase of the building process seemed to be critical, and caulking was no exception. Caring for the large and often leaky seams of *Sunalee* had provided me with some experience, so I didn't approach the job as a complete novice. In addition Julio, who for years had maintained a big wooden sloop, had stopped by to give me tips on the process. The fluffy cotton was pounded in firmly until it became, in effect, a single strand which filled all but the outer eighth inch of the seam. Above the water line, the packed cotton was primed with enamel paint, below with a mixture of pine tar, creosote and paint thinner. The remaining gap would be filled flush to the surface with linseed oil putty.

There were several hundred feet of seams to caulk, and the process stretched out over a two-week period. I learned to feed the cotton and hold the iron in my left hand and keep a bit of rhythm with the mallet in my right. Without a need for power tools, the generator noise was eliminated and I could keep the tape recorder playing nearby. The music didn't speed the process since I had to stop occasionally for Pavarotti to hit the high notes and for the barbershop quartet to cry out the final chord, but it did help me balance my perspective.

Two security officers filled me in on the new project. The VOA signal would be picked up by satellite and then rebroadcast through two powerful transmitters using medium-wave frequencies for long-distance transmission. The large size of the clearing was necessary because the plan called for the antennas to be mounted on twenty, tall towers. Power for the operation would be generated onsite. The programming, primarily in Spanish, would originate in the United States. The antennas would redirect the signal to Honduras and Nicaragua.

Listening to shortwave radio had been part of our evening routine for the previous twelve years and we were familiar with the broadcasts of VOA as well as those of Britain, Canada, Cuba, The Netherlands, Austria, and several other countries. Each station had special programs we enjoyed, and each had its own bias when reporting news. We concluded the most accurate information came from countries not directly involved in the issue. During the Viet Nam war, Radio Hanoi and VOA reports were so extremely different it was hard to believe they were describing the same battle. Radio Canada gave a more credible, third perspective.

VOA had some good programs, including a great jazz show, and except on issues involving the military, we trusted the accuracy of their news coverage. We would, however, often comment on what we called punch line reports where the news item was followed with a final sentence that put a particular spin on the issue. In addition to providing the news, VOA's purpose was to express the U.S. government's perspective to foreign countries; it was not aimed at entertaining its own citizens living abroad.

On one broadcast, a U.S. Information Agency official had described the charter of VOA: to give the news accurately, to project a balance of American thought and institutions, and to clearly present the policies of the U.S. government. If our understanding of Latin American politics was anywhere close to being accurate, American thought and the policies of the government in our region were two different things; the programmers had a real challenge.

We believed most Americans supported the democratic institutions that promoted freedom of religion, a free press, an independent judiciary and the right to dissent. Part of U.S. foreign aid had been aimed at improving the living standards of the world's people and we had known a number of Peace Corps volunteers who were attempting to bring this about.

On the other hand, foreign policy in Latin America had focused on "protecting American interests." Many of those interests were established before and during the world wars when Americans were concentrating on keeping their own freedom and had little time to worry about the freedoms of a few countries in Latin America. A kind of privatized colonialism had developed.

The American-owned United Fruit Company was established in Guatemala near the beginning of the twentieth century and had vast holdings throughout the region. In 1954 the democratically-elected government of Guatemalan President, Jacobo Arbenz, who was in the process of instituting agrarian reform that would threaten the fruit company, was toppled by U.S.-backed forces.

In 1922 Anaconda Copper, also American-owned, established the largest copper mine in the world in Chile.

In 1973, democratically-elected Salvador Allende nationalized the mine. With the facilitation of the CIA, his government was replaced by the military dictatorship of Augusto Pinochet.

To "secure the property of American citizens," Nicaragua was occupied by U.S. Marines from 1912 to 1933, and the bloody dictatorship of the Somoza family enjoyed an alliance with the American government for over forty years.

In 1984 the International Court of Justice ruled that the United States had violated international law by giving military support to the contra rebels. The present Nicaraguan government had been voted in by a landslide in elections that were declared free and fair by the majority of the international observers. Therefore, the Reagan administration was continuing to violate international and national law to overthrow the Sandinista government and the Belizean VOA station was one part of that policy. We were aware that in recent times the Soviet Union had also become a player in the region and that we were immersed in a worldwide cold war, but the older and more fundamental contest was not capitalism vs. communism but rather capitalism vs. democracy. Many of the points scored on the side of democracy had been cancelled by actions of the U.S. government. Yes, VOA had their work cut out for them to meld American thought with the U.S. government's actions and for the first time since the bulldozers started clearing I felt some sympathy.

Tina and I have never been able to shake our idealism. Though we no longer expect from our government, the things we were promised in our junior-high civics class, we still can't handle outright deception. After coming to Belize we had a few years where we could ignore this dichotomy in the national character, but now it had caught up with us and we found ourselves in the midst of the war of isms—we hoped we could face it like warriors.

COLOR

Our world is full of color,
in the seas, in flowers and sky
In people's ways of living
and the thoughts of when they die,

'Til some ism comes along
and paints it all the same
In an effort to exploit,
what e'er the ism's name.

When we question broadly,
our varied points of view
Add flavor to the dish of life,
like small chunks in a stew.

I like life in living color,
not grayed with ism's paint;
So it's likely you will find me
someplace where isms ain't.

KGS

12

~~~

May 1985

BETTER THAN GOLD

It had rained an inch or so in the night, but the sun rose into a clear sky. Ramón had stopped for a visit, his rubber boots caked with mud. He didn't make a lot of small talk: he only said something when he had something to say, but he was skilled at getting someone else to talk, and he was a keen listener.

"Look like they gone plow up the road."

"Yeah, it never was good, but at least we could walk it in the wet—lone mud now."

It had been a dirt road left over from a defunct resort attempt on the old Lukas property (now a part of VOA) that had sodded in; the overhanging trees had shaded it much of the day and made it a comfortable walking trail. We were careful to drive on it only when it was dry. But since most of it was on a public easement, we couldn't stop the bulldozers from using it when they began clearing the VOA site. "I don't know who will walk through that muck to buy our bowls." This was a serious concern; the tourist season was over and we couldn't expect orders from the gift shops. We counted on walk-in customers in the off-season.

"I hear they are putting in a new radio station. Radio Belize not always clear so that's good."

"Better study your Spanish then; this is supposed to be for the people in Honduras and Nicaragua."

"Betta it was a canning factory. I hear plenty jobs in that kind a place and we got lota fruits in this distric'."

In Punta Gorda the number-one criterion for evaluating a project was determining how many jobs it would create. Except for government employees, most people lived on a subsistence level. In the rural villages, farming could support large families, and even after Ramón had moved to town, a new baby kept arriving every year or two. But he no longer had a farm to help feed them and each new family member required more food, clothes, and school books.

Most people saw progress in "getting rid of the bush," and VOA certainly met this condition. Even the national anthem directed Belizeans to "clear the land," with the promise that they would no longer need to be "hewers of wood." In both regards, my sentiments ran in the opposite direction. I grew up on the Montana prairie, part of the Great American Desert, where trees were almost sacred. Ramón grew up in the rain forest where it was a constant struggle to keep the forest from taking over his family compound. Since the time he was big enough to swing a machete, he had spent part of each year cutting down a portion of the forest to make his *milpa* (farming plot). Before there were so many people, this slash and burn system had been ecologically sound and very productive, but now the land was being overworked. When the VOA clearing was complete, he would need to walk farther from his home to gather firewood, but I could expect no commiseration regarding the destruction of the forest. I saw beauty in the trees and wonder in the myriad of creatures the forest supported; he saw the practicality of a clearing and the productivity of a cornfield.

In addition, few Belizeans shared my satisfaction at being a wood worker. Certainly there were skilled boat builders and carvers in the country, but generally, people seemed to prefer office jobs. Historically, one branch of the Belizean family tree was made up of pirates who reluctantly slogged through the swamps to cut logwood when the robbing and plundering business was slow. Another branch was made up of Africans who were dragged from their homes and brought to Belize to slave in the mahogany industry. A prejudice against manual labor is quite understandable.

"Plenty dry firewood." Ramón was referring to the huge windrows of brush and trees the 'dozers were pushing up to prepare for burning. "Well, I gone look for a stick to carry home." He shouldered his axe and started down the trail. He exuded calmness and courage, making the most of the cards life dealt him; I needed to take a page from his book.

"We can't run our fence on the line without clearing at least 30 feet on your side, otherwise, your trees will overhang it," the project manager stated.

That's your problem, was the unstated comment that came to my mind. We were looking over the site plans for the VOA compound. Suddenly, I realized this was *his* creative project, a thousand times bigger than mine but similar: a set of plans, a budget (probably also limited), and the challenge of getting good materials. In addition he had labor issues, a time deadline and most importantly, he would probably get fired if he failed. Boatbuilding seemed simple in comparison.

"Your plan shows a fence running along your southern boundary. Maybe you haven't looked at that area yet but that's all swamp. I doubt your bulldozers can work in there, and even if you clear it, your fence will be in water most of the year." I was making an attempt to set aside my bellicose attitude—being cooperative came more naturally anyway.

"Well, I'll check it out. If we can't make use of that area, there won't be any reason to run the fence along your place."

Feeling some relief, I added, "Our northern boundary shouldn't be a problem since it has a road easement that will separate our trees from your fence." We had a cup of coffee, and I returned to the shop with an order for a set of bowls he would take back to his wife.

To build on this budding relationship with VOA management, I decided to start on the bowls right away. Also our desperate need for cash was, as the British say, not an inconsiderable factor.

I took the chainsaw back to my rosewood pile behind the shop. The pale-yellow sapwood of the small trunks and branches had played its role in protecting the heart during the year-long seasoning process but was now getting rotten. I crosscut three, seven-inch sections from a ten-inch log then put a heavy latex sealer on to prevent checking of the exposed grain. On the band saw, I ripped out a block on each side of the heart crack and then sawed each into a disc to mount on my lathe. All the sapwood was cut away during the shaping process leaving me with a flaw-free bowl two inches by six. I would spend about an hour and a half cutting (including numerous tool sharpening), sanding and polishing each of the six bowls. I had, by that time, turned several thousand pieces, still I had to concentrate on my work or a careless move would send the bowl flying across the shop. Yet, I only had to raise my eyes to see the boat twenty feet away, and a portion of my brain was planning how and where to put the interior blocking.

With the hull smoothed and caulked, temporary cross spalls had been put in place and the molds had been removed leaving the hull open. What a beautiful sight! It was a study in curves and symmetry—the port side a mirror image of the starboard. Completing the hull made the structure look like a boat, and being able to move around inside gave it the feel of one. Seeing the planking, ribs, butt blocks, and floor timbers, in relation to one another, was proof that the puzzle was finally coming together.

The outer layer was the planking, and now the middle layer was being completed with pieces that fit between the frames. Amidships, a pair of blocks was placed where the engine water and exhaust valves would be located. Another pair was positioned forward for the toilet inlet and outlet valves. Each block was shaped to fit snugly against the planking and the adjacent frames. They were smoothed, sealed with pine tar, bedded and fastened in place.

We had access to quality, reasonably-priced wood in large dimensions, but all metals had to be imported and were very expensive; our budget encouraged us to be innovative. Normally heavy straps of bronze or stainless steel would be fastened to the hull sides to anchor the shrouds, the support wires for the masts; we carved our chain plates from large beams of Santa Maria. They were placed between frames and extended two feet below the deck level and one foot above. They were shaped to the same angle the shrouds would take, and the heads were rounded and bored to accept the tensioning lines.

Up forward, the knight's heads, vertical timbers on each side of the stem, were made of *Bethabara* and holes were bored through them where the anchor lines would run. The extreme hardness of this wood made a metal hawse pipe unnecessary. Blocking between the frames at the sheerline would accept bolts from the cap and rub rails. Each piece, whether small or large, had to be shaped and smoothed on every surface, sealed, bedded and fastened into place. Throughout the boatbuilding process, the time a particular step required was based more on the number of pieces and steps involved than on size.

As I hustled to finish the manager's order so we could buy our week's groceries, I chuckled over a comment Ramón had made. "The black people say because you build this boat, you got plenty of money; you jus' act like us poor people." His kidding and sense of humor slid easily across the cultural boundaries and his timing had been perfect—I only had five dollars in my pocket and I would use it to pay his teenage son who was weeding our garden. An expected check from a gift shop had not arrived and we had just returned from town with only two days' groceries and fuel. At the time I was unable to appreciate the irony of his comment, and a verse for a poem I would later call *Big Words* came to mind:

> *Before I was in business*
> *I'd be "broke" sometimes, you know,*
> *But now when there's no money*
> *The problem's just "cash flow"!*

White people were expected to have plenty of money, and most did, based on Belizean standards. We were asked, several times, to be godparents and to take on the expenses of confirmations and school books. Fortunately, from a financial perspective, the local priest did not allow non-Catholics to play this role. Still, we tried to help out when we could. I used to explain how poor we were when I had to turn down a request for employment or a "loan" until, one day, I heard the response, "Man, you got bags of excuses." I realized I was being misleading. It was true we had very little cash but we were rich in self-confidence, a critical element for any innovative project—one that no amount of money could buy.

But confidence alone wouldn't pay our expenses, replenish our diminishing physical reserves or provide emotional stability. An offer of relief came from an unexpected source—our daughter Christie and son-in-law-Carlos. They had grown up together in Belize and after their marriage had moved to Dallas to build up a nest egg. Tina responded enthusiastically to their offer:

May 2, 1985
Dear Christie & Carlos,
 Thank you for the wonderful and generous invitation so we can go on vacation with you. It does seem like we need a break from this situation. Some distance might help us have a clearer perspective on the activities at the back of the property. As it is Dad's blood pressure is high and he is working long hours.
 It sounds like you have a whirlwind tour planned to see everyone! It will be wonderful to see Grandma again. I miss her letters now that she can't see to write. And it would help if we could see Scott and be sure he is well situated.
 We had not anticipated that this project would take us so long, thus keeping us without resources to travel. So, yes, we will join you. Let us know when you will be leaving. We will get a caretaker.
 I can hardly wait!
 Love, Mama

13

~~~

August 1985

NO TURNING BACK

We returned from our visit to the States with a fresh perspective. The hull looked beautiful in the sweep of her lines and in her symmetry, and she was big! I felt uplifted as I thought of the skills we had acquired. We had accomplished a lot but it was clear there was a long way to go.

Despite my frustration with the slow pace of the project the eventual launching was a foregone conclusion—there was no turning back or stopping. Quitting would mean leaving a useless object to rot in the forest—a monument to our lack of follow-through, inexperience and our ultimate failure. Unacceptable! And there was no sense trying to speed the process by taking shortcuts; we had to give our best to each step for our inexperience would create enough errors of its own.

Charles Borden spoke frequently, in his book *Sea Quest,* about the lure of the sea and described the various types of craft that have evolved through eons of human experience. When I questioned the wisdom of what we were doing, I had only to read a chapter in his book to know that this type of insanity has gone on for a long time. From the basic craft carved from a log to supertankers, humankind, on every shoreline of the world has found ways to move across the water.

I now realized it was not just the call of the sea that compelled me to keep on; if so I would have been happy with a plastic tub for a boat. To see a lovely wooden craft floating at anchor or under sail spoke to me at some artistic level—building a yearning that became a physical pressure in my chest. But what a strange phenomenon to happen; I am from an ancestry of teachers, preachers and farmers. I didn't discover sailing until I was twenty-eight years old. Except for an attempt to water ski on a lake or swim along a beach, I had had no real connection to the sea or vessels of any kind. I couldn't help but wonder where this dormant love affair came from. It was as if the sea experience was necessary for me to become whole.

I chose this world of wooden boats as my own and I nurtured these yearnings until they became my reality. As a child I was captivated with tales of tropical sailing adventures. Now I devoured any real-life stories and even maritime historical fiction. I became immersed in the details of all aspects of boats—even engines, propellers and electronics. It seems I was selectively bringing part of my culture with me, for we were, in an oblique way, part and parcel of the current revival of craftsmanship and wooden boatbuilding that was occurring in North America.

Now that *Sunalee* was gone, I felt restless, yet I knew this phase of the building would require focus and patience for there were many, many, small pieces that had to be shaped and finished before that empty hull was completed inside and out. *Just one day at a time*, I told myself—I sensed she was waiting patiently for us to continue; her essence and the rewards from the process itself were leading us on. If ever I needed my inner eye, it was at that moment, to see our way clear of the mental chaos that had invaded our lives with the advent of the VOA project. I wanted to think on a higher level, to concentrate on this wonderful opportunity to be a part of humankind's cease-less endeavor to create.

Kirby never questioned his commitment to the boat project, but he missed sailing too. Jumping ahead and building a dinghy that we would need later would at least give us something to sail. We still had the plans for the one we had built for *Sunalee*. The design was simple and, using two sheets of our lofting plywood, it went together quickly. With several coats of white enamel and a stripe of blue trim along the gunnels, she would match the ketch. She could carry a good load so we rowed her into the market when the wind was calm and sailed back home with the sea breeze. Kirby was disappointed in her sailing abilities and dubbed her the *Oardeal*, but even that brief sail would bring up my spirits.

He finished what he called the inner layer of the hull—the fore and aft (lengthwise) members: the clamp, which tied all the frame heads together like the wall plate on a house, the bilge straps, which did the same where the curve of the hull was greatest, and the ceiling, which sheathed the inside of the frames between the floor timbers and the clamp.

Trapped fresh water and high humidity spell doom for wooden boats, so ventilation and drainage were major considerations throughout the boat construction. Kirby made sure there were no dead air spaces and his goal was that every drop of water, no matter where it entered the hull, would quickly find its way to the bilge where it could be pumped out.

With the longitudinal members fastened to the transom frame, we could, at last, close up the end of the boat. Thick planks were necessary to give strength to this flat and vulnerable area and two-inch, light-weight cedar was the choice of wood. To avoid its well-known characteristic of reacting with galvanized fastenings, we stepped back in time a few centuries and used trunnels (tree nails) to fasten the planks to the frame. By putting in hardwood dowels with tiny wedges at each end, we were working entirely with natural materials and it gave us a special satisfaction.

Most metals have a finite lifetime in warm salt water, so fastening the whole boat with wooden dowels might have been the best for longevity. But Kirby thought it was so time-consuming, we might be too old to sail by the time the boat was finished. From our reading and personal experience, we knew the biggest mistake would be to use a variety of metals that would react with each other, so, except for the transom planks and interior joinery, we used quality, hot-dipped-galvanized-iron fastenings throughout. They were strong, fairly easily obtained, proven in local conditions, moderately priced and should be fairly long lasting.

Choosing the kind of bolts, screws and nails to use was like many other decisions on the boat project, a compromise—longevity and re-sale value on one hand, cost, availability and construction time on the other. An artist can make a drawing on the ceiling of a church or on a napkin; it depends whether it is the process or the product that is more important. We wanted the boat strong; her integrity was critical, but wood is a biodegradable material and we accepted the fact that the boat's life would have a limit. We were building the vessel for ourselves, not for sale, and ideally the wood, the fastenings and the owners would all have about the same working lifetime.

The beams not only support the deck and the cabin tops, they hold the sides of the boat together and must absorb the thrust of the masts while sailing; careful joinery is critical. *WoodenBoat* published an article on deck framing by Bud McIntosh that we discovered just as we arrived at that phase of construction. He was as practical in his techniques as Culler was in his designs and they shared the commonality of simplicity. Bud was a builder and he didn't believe in making complex joints where they weren't necessary. But the features that set his articles apart from any other how-to books we had read were the clarity of his writing and the illustrations by Sam Manning. Kirby enjoyed the work, but, because it often had to take a back seat to lathe work, the process stretched out over many weeks.

Kirby and I had been preparing beam stock by running some big timbers through the planer when Bill arrived on his four-wheeler. He unstrapped a 70 or 80 pound shapeless chunk of rosewood burl and lugged it on to the shop floor. Bill had been contracted to erect the VOA antenna towers.

"This burl came from Frank and I was hoping you could turn a bowl from it." It was a gnarly looking thing that had wrapped itself around a tree and had a big "V" notch where it had been cut free. Burls have the extreme hardness and density of the parent tree but a gorgeous tight and swirly grain. Kirby had used it for tea cup and stein handles, and even buttons and had turned bearings and pulleys from it for our own tools. We had read that burls were growths caused by "prolific budding" usually as a result of "injury due to freezing." Only God was old enough to remember the last freeze in our area.

Kirby studied it for a while and said, "We should be able to get five or six small bowls from the edges and a nice serving bowl from the middle."

"No, I want one big bowl—the biggest you can get out of it."

"I can only turn 11-inch diameter on my lathe," Kirby responded.

"Frank said you would figure something out, but if you can't, I don't want it cut into a bunch of small pieces."

Kirby spent the next hour measuring the burl and studying his lathe. He finally got his courage up and began butchering the burl with the chain saw. The next morning was spent remaking the bed on his lathe and building a temporary tool rest. He estimated the weight of the turning blank at 35 pounds—quite a challenge for this $29 kit tool and its washing-machine motor.

Bill stopped back in a couple of days with two rolls of aluminum-coated-steel cable—a bit oversized but plenty for our mast shrouds and stays. If it could support the 180-foot towers at VOA, it would be more than strong enough for our purposes; we were ecstatic.

By the end of the week, the bowl, almost a basin, 16 inches by 6 inches was done—one flawless piece of wood. Using the branding iron made by Kirby's brother, our logo was burned into the bottom. When Bill saw the bowl he declared it a gift fit for a queen. It had been an exchange that left everyone pleased. Kirby put his versatile little lathe back together with affection.

14
~~~

August 1985

MUY PROBLEMA

The VOA site was a muddy morass. Only foreigners would try to do construction at the height of the rainy season. Our friend Frank, who had sawn the lumber for our frames and decking, knew an opportunity when he saw one. It was far too wet for timbering, so he converted his log skidders into construction tractors and leased them to VOA. Being some of the few vehicles that could operate in the quagmire, they bored footings, mixed cement and transported materials.

Frank had led a colorful life. In Belize he had piloted and crashed a small airplane, stolen back a vessel that had been stolen from him, had set up and run the largest sawmill in the district, had gained and lost a fortune or two and was, at the moment, setting up a new furniture factory. He spent much of his time on the VOA site, keeping his skidders going, and he stopped by often to check on our boat's progress.

"I was over in Guatemala last week and saw a little Perkins diesel you might be interested in."

"I hear Perkins builds a good machine, but they don't make a hand-start engine." Kirby had literature on every imaginable small marine diesel. Very few could operate without an electrical system, and Kirby was adamant about not having to depend on batteries.

"Well, this one has a hand crank, a marine transmission and nothing electric."

Kirby and I had gone over the numbers a dozen times and concluded we couldn't afford an engine, but we were building in such a way it could be installed later.

At the end of the week, Frank stopped back. "You've probably heard that the quetzal devalued, and the Guatemalan government has frozen the retail prices on everything. I just bought a planer for a third of what it would have cost last month."

Kirby was all ears, "I suppose that Perkins is gone by now."

"It is still there for $1500 if you have U.S. cash. It looks like the same three-cylinder engine they use in the Massey Ferguson tractor, so you should be able to buy parts for it here."

That's how it happened. We broke the CD we had from *Sunalee's* sale, the money that was to let us work fulltime on the boat. Shortly after a friend from the U.S. brought the cash down, we boarded the ferry to Puerto Barrios.

It was rainy and dark by the time we and our travelling companions, Delly and Alvin, got through immigration. We sloshed to a near-by hotel, the Caribeña, where most Belizeans stayed. The hotel was full so we hailed another taxi. Delly and a Punta Gorda teacher with her children dived into the small vehicle out of the rain. I wedged myself into the back seat, but there was no room for Kirby and Alvin. The door slammed behind me, and the taxi drove off into the night. We didn't even know which hotel we were going to. I panicked—how would Kirby be able to follow? I realized traveling in a group was a lot more complex than going on our own.

The next hotel was also full, and we went on to look for another. I was getting more and more nervous. In the rainy night with all the lights and traffic I couldn't tell if Kirby and Alvin were behind us or not. The taxi pulled into the next hotel, and we all emerged. In a few minutes another taxi pulled in. As Kirby climbed out I flew into his arms. He appeared as worried as I felt; a long look into each other's eyes subdued our panicky nerves.

"Man, that's a bad way to begin a trip!" he exclaimed once we were alone in our room. "The rooms are scarce because there is a conference in town. There are only a few hotels, so I would have found you eventually, but I knew you would be anxious."

"Anxious? I was frightened out of my mind! And you have my passport in your pocket! We have to plan better than this."

"Yes, I'd rather we made our own mistakes—together."

The next morning Alvin led us to the bus station. He had traveled here with Frank so knew about the transport system and spoke a little Spanish. But figuring out how to transact business was going to be another issue; the country was in turmoil due to its currency devaluation, and the government was trying to avoid financial chaos by freezing the price on all items in stock and restricting exchange of dollars and quetzals.

Our arrival in Guatemala City in mid-afternoon gave us time to get to the dealership to examine the engine. Kirby liked it on sight—perhaps because, as a child on the Montana farm, he was familiar with tractor engines. Its simplicity and grey paint made it the ugly duckling in a showroom of glistening, expensive equipment. The salesman tried his best to sell Kirby a different engine.

The little Perkins had a history. It seems it was acquired when this business had bought out the Perkins dealer soon after the damaging 1978 earthquake. It had languished for seven years in their storage room, but now with the financial crunch, the store was liquidating every unnecessary item to avoid an excessive inventory tax. They had welded the crank mechanism, cleaned it up and given it a fresh coat of paint. Several of these engines had been ordered as part of a program to provide economical power for work boats; this one had never been picked up. It was just what Kirby wanted; it was hefty, developed its power at low rpm's and could be started by hand.

"I will think about it," Kirby told the salesman.

Alvin planned to buy a motor and generator from the same dealer. He was going to exchange his cash "on the street"—illegal, but supposedly more profitable. Kirby had been wavering between the simplicity and safety of exchanging money at the dealership or getting a better rate on the street. His inherited tendencies for good deals won out once he knew of Alvin's plan. Delly and I were nothing but apprehensive that night as we followed our men and their "contact" into a side street tailor shop. The contact had a pistol on his hip. Delly began hyper-ventilating and whimpering now and again. I was a bit numb as I blocked out the possible outcomes this situation could lead to— finally I took Delly by the arm and led her outside. She saw the contact come out and go across the street to a phone box—now, she began to panic in earnest. I kept shushing her as people on the street turned to look at us. I couldn't know what they were thinking, and it didn't matter as long as they didn't attract the police to our situation. The truth was all four of us were essentially babes *from* the woods.

Finally, the men joined us with Alvin shoving a wad of quetzals into his pocket. We kept looking over our shoulders, hoping we had not attracted enough attention to put some nervy thief on our trail. We decided to go back to the hotel in a roundabout way acting like tourists. In an ice cream shop I turned to Kirby, "This isn't exactly the kind of outing I had in mind." Of course, it was intended to be a business trip, but since I so seldom left the Point any break had potential as a holiday. So far, this trip didn't fit into that category.

The small, box-like, unventilated room in the multistoried hotel gave me claustrophobia while the traffic in the halls all night, along with moaning, groaning and the occasional scream from adjacent rooms let us know we hadn't chosen a hotel for families. It was a long, restless and mostly sleepless night. Delly told me she barricaded the door with a chest of drawers when someone punched a hole in one of their walls. We were all in a wretched state in the morning.

It didn't get better. The large equipment was purchased by both men, and shipping arrangements were made. The monies were paid in quetzals, and the dealer upped the price because we hadn't paid in U.S. dollars. So, the night's escapades had cost in cash and goodwill as well as in nervous sweat—an effective cure for the "good deal" syndrome. Now we had to hurry back the 200 miles to Puerto Barrios.

"Wait a minute! We haven't been to the big *mercado* yet. I want to look for some *tipico* blouses and skirts."

"Sorry, Love, the money's nearly gone, and we have to meet the truck and find a way to get this stuff home."

"But all I have seen are parts stores and a brothel!"

"Next time," and he hurried off to join Alvin at the bus ticket stand.

At the harbor the customs officials gave us another set of bad nerves as they studied our noticeably-low-valued receipts. Not knowing what to do with us and our purchases, they insisted we go back to the city for export permits. We finally figured out that the *mordida* system (cash tips) that once kept everything flowing smoothly was askew because of the financial situation; no one was going to make any risky decisions. We were stuck.

Locals told us that nothing was being exported right then and to let it rest awhile—the system would eventually straighten itself out, and if not, there would always be the "back door." We hated leaving behind our biggest investment yet, but we were emotionally strung out and exhausted. Accepting a friend's offer to store the engine in his yard would let us recuperate and give us time to figure out what to do next.

The place was not done with me yet. Hoping I would be somewhat appeased, we wandered through the local market before heading over to buy tickets for the ferry. Having taken a left turn while everyone else took a right into the maze of the building's interior, I continued halfway around the block before I realized I had lost my companions. Knowing the folly of looking for them in the warren of inside stalls, I sat down on a bench and waited. And I waited, and waited. Suddenly there before me was a tall hulk of a man wearing only a loincloth, bells on ankles and wrists and assorted necklaces of carved images. Keeping a rhythm, he chanted first in my direction then in another—his stench assaulted my already queasy stomach. The vibrations coming off this person felt like an attack. My head became dizzy. No one else was paying him any attention. "Where *is* Kirby?" I muttered, and once again started sliding into panic. From a hot flash, from fear, or both, I started sweating just as Kirby came around the far corner of the block-size building.

"Where did you go?"

"I thought you were right behind me. I didn't see you turn."

Irrationally I wanted to blame him for not watching out for me better, but it had been my fault for gawking at all the merchandise. I didn't feel like a sophisticated international traveler so much as a middle-aged, menopausal woman totally out of her element. Later, walking down to the ferry I was taken aback when Delly said, "Oh, Miss Tina, I thought someone had abducted you! You were so cool sitting there all by yourself; I would have been so frightened."

Back home, Caleb, our faithful canine companion, greeted us with affectionate forbearance. We continued our progress on the deck framing and, of course, the daily lathe work, but Kirby was preoccupied with the Perkins. He made several phone calls to Guatemala—the situation there had not stabilized. A week after our return he wrote in his diary:

"After wrestling with the export problem, I finally decided to take it on as a challenge and a learning experience for entering foreign ports in the future and feel better for it. It has been a worrisome, nagging thing up to now."

Three days later he took the ferry back to Puerto Barrios alone, and I began my vigil. The time went by, and I had no word from him. I feared he had been locked up in some terrible Guatemalan jail. Near midnight of the fourth day the sound of an outboard engine woke me with a start. Caleb had started barking his *people* bark. I climbed out of bed and ran downstairs. I listened intently until I heard, "Tina, I'm here." I slid back the bolt on the stout wooden door and a dripping, bedraggled figure stepped inside. "Pedro dropped me a bit down the shore. We have the engine." He hugged me tight then began stripping off his wet clothing while telling me the details of his adventure.

When I arrived in Puerto Barrios I told Juan my intentions to go through the proper channels—to get export approval even if it meant going back to Guatemala City. He told me to avoid the city, they are having riots there. The president declared a halt to all foreign currency exchange. He thought I might get in serious trouble explaining how we had paid for it. He advised me to get the engine out anyway I could. Pedro, (a Belizean fisherman we knew) was in town selling his catch and Juan suggested I talk to him. He knows his way around and I knew he could get it out if anyone could.

Pedro assured me it was no problem, but it might take a couple of days to get the paperwork done. So I tried to relax and make a holiday of it. I wasn't very successful. I walked every street of the town, read a novel and spent hours waiting for Pedro to give a daily progress report and to receive a few more dollars for entertaining the officials. Of course he had to drink along with them. Following his instructions, I hired a truck this morning and took the engine to a small dock at the end of the market and loaded it into a beamy, 30-foot dory. There was a small crane available to do the job. Pedro met me there at sundown and we cast off.

There was quite a chop after we left the port, and we were taking on a little water over the bow. I only had a half Clorox bottle to bail with, so I kept at it pretty steady. We had the sea to ourselves for about an hour and then picked up the lights of a large cruiser that Pedro figured was the navy patrol boat. First there was just a red light but then we saw the green one too and knew he was heading towards us. We were a mile off the Guatemalan coast heading northwest toward Punta Gorda. Pedro changed course to keep more distance between us and the cruiser. He assured me that our papers were in order, but I had my doubts. The owner of this rented dory was only temporarily convinced too. He had intercepted us as we left the harbor and wanted to take his dory back. Pedro had assured him all was tranquilo and after receiving a beer he let us go on. A few feet ahead of me sat the crate containing the diesel engine—its value suddenly seemed minimal compared to my freedom. I was really wondering why I had let myself get involved in this shady operation.

We were undoubtedly showing on the cruiser's radar, and Pedro again changed course slightly to make it appear that we were not planning to leave Guatemalan waters but were just on our way to the port of Livingston. He had explained this as his alternative plan, one that wouldn't require him to be in possession of "a lot of papers." The fact my passport showed I had just stamped out of the country and my engine receipt gave Punta Gorda as my address would hardly have supported that scenario.

After a few minutes the green light disappeared, and the cruiser gradually moved away as it continued on its patrol. I heard Pedro sigh; I know he had done this plenty of times, but he was worried too. An hour later we cleared Cocoli Point and could safely make our turn toward home. Farther off shore the sea was rough and I had to bail in earnest. But *it is a lot easier to deal with Nature's challenges than with the complexities of civilization.*"

I handed him a towel, ran up for a flannel blanket, and returned to wrap it around him. I heated water for a bath and a cup of Milo to warm him—slowly he wound down. Yawning, he gripped the blanket, picked up the towel and went in to bathe, my words following him, "I thought I would have to go looking for you tomorrow."

"Pedro will come in the morning to take me and the engine into immigration and customs. I hope this damned thing runs," were his last words as he dragged himself up the stairs to bed.

I poured myself a cup of chamomile tea and sat down at the table; finally in relief and gratitude I let the tears flow. Sick and feverish with some germ I picked up while in Guatemala, with swollen glands and vile chest congestion, I had been a bit frightened at being alone. I tried to continue the boat work and house chores in some semblance of normal life only to slip and fall. A bad headache and nausea told me I had a slight concussion. During this very sorry state, the fate of both Kirby and the engine hung in limbo and the tension came out in a terrible back pain. Now that he had returned safely all the pain was miraculously gone. The terrible days of worry were over, but I knew they were indelibly written on my memory.

Muttering to myself, "I too, hope this damned engine runs," I climbed into bed and snuggled against his warm body.

Once again all was right with my world.

15
~~~

September 1985-May 1986

ONE'S PERSPECTIVE

After our Guatemalan experiences, it was a relief to return to the shop where the buzz of the saw, the whine of the drill, and the scream of the planer spoke a language we understood, and the rules, since we made them ourselves, were clear and easy to follow.

A floating object experiences very little stress compared to one that is being propelled though the water. In a power boat the engine beds and the timbers they are fastened to must be very strong to transmit the thrust of the propellers to the hull. In a wind driven boat the thrust of the sail is transmitted to the hull through the mast and the standing and running rigging. Weakness in any of these components is to be avoided. Each mast is essentially an arrow pointed at the bottom of the boat; the hull is the bow and the shrouds the bow string.

To strengthen the hull we put a pair of large, vertical knees on each side between beam and rib in the area having the most stress—where the masts pass through the deck. The holes for the masts were cut through heavy blocking, the partners, and were larger than the mast dimensions to allow for wedging. The deck itself was braced with several lodging knees to keep it from racking in the horizontal direction. These knees were laminated from thin strips of Santa Maria. For further strengthening, long bolts were run between the carlins and the clamps to stiffen the side decks. The builder strives to give his hull integrity— the kind that allows a discarded light bulb to float through hurricane conditions without damage.

The support member for the foot of the mast, the step, keeps the tensioned mast from going through the bottom of the boat. A socket was cut in the fore knee that would accept the tenon of the main mast. The mizzen mast step was a bridge that allowed the propeller shaft to pass below it. It was fashioned from a noble piece of hard pine and supported by extra heavy floor timbers.

With knees and deck beams in place, the framing of the cockpit began. Pete Culler designed our boat as a coastal cruiser, not weaker than an ocean sailer, but with different features. A large and functional cockpit could be employed since there would be little chance of an ocean storm wave breaking over the stern and filling it. As a sailor and a builder, as well as a designer, Pete knew what made a coastal boat function well and how to build simply. The cockpit floor was a complete lower deck which ran from side to side and from the transom to the aft cabin. The forward corners drained directly through hull scuppers without piping, and the large areas under the side and aft decks were easily accessible. Air beneath the cockpit circulated naturally upward to vent above the sheer clamp. Framing was similar to the main deck itself. It was simple, strong and functional.

The cockpit and the deck were planked in the traditional manner. Strips of Santa Maria 1¼ X 1¾ were sprung into place matching the curve of the hull sides. A broad king plank was laid down the middle, and a wide covering board along the outboard edge, its scarf joints bolted together, completed the decking. Since it would be sheathed, the seams were not caulked. If water found its way under the deck covering, it seemed better to let it pass on through, even onto the captain's bunk, than to trap it and initiate rot.

Carlos and Christie took leave from their Dallas jobs for a visit home in February of 1986 to check on the property they had purchased adjacent to ours and also to check on Carlos's mother and on us. We had assured them that we were doing fine—that we had made the adjustment to having VOA as our neighbor. Tina admitted in our letters that I was having occasional chest pains and my blood pressure was high but said it was probably a reaction to something I was eating and from pushing too hard on the boat work. The logical solution was to ease up a little and refrain from eating green peppers.

A few days after their arrival, Carlos and I put on our boots and hiked over to the VOA compound. His father had been our mentor and friend. As a snake doctor and herbalist, he had taught his son the skills of close observation and critical thinking. Carlos could usually see, in both a literal and a figurative sense, details I had overlooked, and I valued his perspective.

The American government continued to conquer the elements by sheer force. Buildings had been erected, all twenty of the tall towers were standing, and the chain link perimeter fence was being completed despite the twelve feet of rain that had fallen during the wet season. Americans accomplished feats that sensible Belizeans would never have attempted and often felt somewhat superior in doing so. Shaking his head, Ramón's comment in the heart of the rainy season had been, "These people spend lot of money and they like to work hard. Why they no wait for the dry?" Still he marveled at the magnitude of the project. The American culture seems to foster ambition, aggressiveness and also a naiveté that Belizean culture does not. It results in the construction of relay stations and sailboats.

The rains had eased off, and a grader was at work smoothing the ruts in the dirt road leading to the headquarters building. I told Carlos of my monthly attempts to get our road replaced. So far all I had gotten was temporary permission to drive through their compound. I introduced Carlos to the chief engineer, Modesto, with whom my relationship could only be described as adversarial. Surprisingly, they seemed to get along quite well. Carlos explained that he would be putting up a concrete structure on his property, and he needed to be able to truck the materials in. Having picked up Carlos' accent, Modesto responded with a friendly phrase in Spanish—the first language for both of them. Then in English for my benefit, "You never had a road there to start with." *I have heard this many times before*, I thought. "But," he said, "we could probably justify putting a maintenance road along there for checking the outside of our fence. I'll try to clear it with my boss."

Carlos saw potential benefits from the presence of VOA and accepted what he had no control over. He *requested* a road and was going to get it. I saw VOA as an invader who had destroyed a portion of my world. I had been *demanding* a road as compensation and had been denied. It is all in one's approach and attitude.

We continued to do specialty craft work for VOA staff and the site contractors. Their business had carried us through the rainy season and had more than offset our loss of walk-in customers. For cash we sold quite a number of regular items, but we did some trading too. Bartering had been an enjoyable aspect of our cottage industry and we had negotiated for a variety of services as well as for materials; on our gypsy trip I had even swapped craft items to the surgeon for a hernia repair.

We traded a set of bowls with a contractor for a roll of half-inch polypropylene line—enough for our running rigging. With the British army doctor we bartered for a first-aid kit, and with their intelligence officer we had exchanged a set of beer steins for a ship's compass. Every sawyer in the district had gone out of his way to supply us with specialty lumber, and most had accepted craft items in lieu of cash. They were some of our most frequent visitors, seemingly proud that their wood was going into the project.

There were numerous friends who stopped by regularly just to give us moral support. Many people went out of their way to help the enterprise along in one way or another. There seemed to be something contagious about the concept of building a boat; perhaps it is because a sailboat, for many, symbolizes ultimate freedom.

We always needed something from the States, and we had our hardware orders sent to anyone who was willing to bring them down; it was rare that a friend or a relative arrived empty handed. Dr. Kerfoot, a medical missionary and one of our rosewood patrons, is a man of small stature and a big heart. He tells a great story of his efforts to look nonchalant as he lifted an overweight box of our fastenings into his plane's overhead compartment, not daring to ask for help. Sailing friends volunteered to bring paint, solvents, and anchor chain. Our long-time friend, Ron, haunted the Florida boat yards for used equipment and specialty tools on our behalf.

Several people had built boats in Belize and shared their innovations with us: like Nick's concrete shoe idea and Jerry's steam-bending experiences. Jerry had spent nine years building a boat similar to ours in Belize City. Julio, a Punta Gorda friend who had built a working sloop back in the '60s, gave me tips on caulking and told me which woods were the most durable. Frank's tip led to our Guatemalan adventures but also to a suitable and inexpensive engine. Dave, an agricultural researcher from the UK, also a sailor, helped us find a sail maker.

Over a "proper" cup of tea we had explained to him our dilemma regarding sails. Tina is a skilled seamstress and had made the sails for *Sunalee*. Buying the materials and having her make sails for the new boat was by far the least expensive of our options. But, since no boats had been built to this plan, its performance was unproven. If she didn't sail well, it might be due to a design error, a builder's mistake or improperly-shaped sails. Getting professionally-made sails would eliminate one of those factors. Dave pointed out that the British pound sterling had recently taken a drop in value. He gave us the name of a sail maker who would do a good job at a reasonable price. After an exchange of letters and the conversion of the last of *Sunalee's* sale money into British pounds, we put in our order. Several weeks later the three sails arrived via parcel post. The customs agent taxed them as rolls of Dacron cloth, resulting in significant savings.

Our craft business kept up with small orders of supplies, but chunks of money were hard to come by. To finance our deck covering and paint we put the old bus up for sale. She was a veteran of several careers: ten years transporting school children and another ten carrying the faithful to church. We brought her out of retirement and for ten more years she made trips between the U.S. and Belize, often carrying boat supplies and tools. Recently I had used her as a log skidder by dragging some salvaged logs off the VOA clearing. A sawyer with a portable mill had been impressed by her capabilities and bought her for a mobile kitchen. She had appreciated almost tenfold in value—we had paid very little for her—and the revenue kept the project going.

The sun was just getting up and we were considering doing the same. It had been a typical jungle night, noisy to the uninitiated, with sounds that we registered but did not find disturbing: the early evening quiet followed by calls of the nighthawks, the irate squawks of the night herons when they missed their thrusts, and the squealing of the kinkajous over infidelity issues. In the early morning hours, the various monkey troops started announcing their territorial claims and at first light the falcon gave a raucous laugh after a long ascending prelude. Toucans followed with unglamorous croaks as if their allotment of beauty had all been squandered on their gaudy bills. Flocks of chachalacas had just started their chorusing when we heard the instrumental version of *Yankee Doodle went to town, riding on a pony*. We both sat up in bed, our brains slowly processing the fact that we were hearing the Voice of America theme song, the prelude to their broadcast day. The forest was eerily silent as the program continued over the site's outdoor loudspeakers.

The towers had been in place for several weeks, a red light on the top of each, and the perimeter lighting was operating. The evening before, we had heard the clang of starting motors and the rumble of the big generators, so the fact they were in business came as no surprise—but to be broadcasting through loudspeakers? Tina said, "They've got to be kidding!" We looked at each other and laughed—it seemed the best way to keep deeper emotions from surfacing.

On many of our local bus trips there would be one person aboard who would play his boom box at high volume. There seemed no malice in the act and Belizeans, being the tolerant people they are, never complained. He may have felt he had something precious and that everyone else would appreciate his generosity in sharing it. Apparently, VOA agreed with this kind of thinking. Naiveté or arrogance; it depends on one's perspective.

16
~~~

June 1986 to August 1986

TORTURE BY STROBE

We toasted the completion of the deck by raising our rosewood goblets full of homemade sorrel wine. It was a slightly bigger celebration than we had had two weeks earlier for our 25th wedding anniversary. Kirby's journal entry explains:

> *June 4, 1986*
> *25th anniv. Celebrated by bingeing on chocolate pudding. Started fastening two pieces of the port covering board. Ran bead of Life Caulk along sheer plank then a thread of cotton wicking . . .*

It was exciting to finally focus on the interior of the boat. At this stage of the process we were not interested in fancy details, or more accurately, we didn't want to spend the time and money on them. We decided we would build a simple and functional interior—trusting that materials and time would come later to finish the work. A boat interior is easier to build before the cabin sides and tops are in place, allowing the materials to be easily moved in and out as needed.

Building cabinetry into a boat's oddly shaped interior where the hull framing is not square, straight, horizontal, or vertical, requires ingenuity and imagination. When designing *Sunalee's* interior, we found that mocking up with scrap material saves a lot of work and prevents many errors. To permanently build in cupboards, bunks, galley and head (toilet) only to discover later they are uncomfortable, inconvenient and maybe even unusable is a painful way to learn a lesson. We cut Masonite into panels that roughly fit the area, and tacked them into place. This allowed us to judge whether our plan would serve us and how it would look and feel. After adjusting for convenient heights and lengths, the same panels would be used as patterns for the permanent construction.

The main cabin was twelve feet long, the width varying from seven feet aft to four feet forward. With the wide bridge deck just outside the companionway, we would have a comfortable living area. A full bulkhead, with a narrow door between the foc'sle and the main saloon, would give support to the cabin top and divide the area into two usable spaces. Pete had designed a half bulkhead between the bunk and the galley area to port with a twin on the starboard side between the bunk and a space for an ice box. They would split the already limited cabin space in half. We decided to build as designed and cut them down later if necessary. A wide plank became a counter for my old two-burner stove.

A few cleats and two-inch strips across the area below the stove would hold several pigtail buckets. These five gallon containers were purchased from the local stores which sold salted pork tails by the pound. They were watertight, cheap and easy to come by. In Belize they served as luggage carriers, bath and laundry tubs and, being insect-proof and generally rat-proof, they were the most reliable containers to store food in. They had served as my main storage ashore and they would do nicely aboard our floating home until something else was devised.

The four large ports would provide good light for the cabin interior. The bunks, tucked under the deck, should be cozy and away from the direct light. Pete emphasized that bunks needed to be amidships and at water level to minimize movement. Beveled cleats were run along the ceiling/sheathing and under the bridge deck into the aft cabin, allowing for two more bunks in that area. For now plywood would serve as bunk surfaces. Along the inboard side of the main bunks we attached a vertical board to keep us in during rolly conditions, which also served as a backrest for the settee bench. The bench was of minimal width so a wide plank would temporarily serve.

The foc'sle is commonly used as a v-berth and/or for storage. For now it was a large open space where we could store extra line and anchors. A bucket in a box would serve for the head. A curtain across the door in the bulkhead would give a degree of privacy.

Cabins of old wooden sailing craft can have an enticing and romantic ambience—a place to enjoy solitude or friendship, a place to write or share yarns. Most of my sailing had been in *lee fat* vessels; I preferred the kind of wide spacious cabins they allowed. Long, narrow, deep cabins made me feel a bit claustrophobic.

Pete also had definite ideas about interiors based on his own experiences. After coming ashore, he had spent many years building and designing for Concordia Yachts. His interiors fit the type of boat he designed—each had the stamp of a traditional workboat—practical and simple. Before and after WWII, Pete and his wife Toni carried freight and chartered along the east coast of the U.S. with their 40-foot yawl, *Spray*. His sailing experiences gave him the opinion that sailboats, even if used only for pleasure, need more than good looks and sailing characteristics; they need to be built strongly and rigged simply so their maintenance and repair costs will be minimized.

It was this perspective, significantly different from most naval architects of his time that attracted us to his designs. His was a bygone era, one that suited us fine. It fit into Belize's history of wooden sailing vessels anchored offshore waiting to load dyewood, mahogany, bananas, sugar, and rum.

We were always up before Yankee Doodle started riding his pony, and since we had 300 yards of forest between us and the compound, the perimeter lights and red tower beacons could not be seen. The rumble of the generators was usually drowned by the sound of the waves on shore. The project engineer had promised to build our road soon. Kirby kept reminding him since it would have to be built before the rains began or not at all. He admitted to being a squeaky wheel but clarified that it wasn't grease he was after but a surface to roll on. We felt we had adjusted to the inevitability of having VOA as a permanent neighbor.

We had gone to bed not long after sundown, exhausted from a typical day of lathing, boat work and chores. Around midnight clouds moved in to cover the sky, a reminder that the dry season was coming to an end. I got up to pee and wondered if I was going crazy—the whole sky was flashing, not intermittently like lightning but rhythmically. Lying back down I noticed Kirby was awake, too. "What is it?" I asked, trying not to sound alarmed.

"It's the strobe lights they put on the towers. Carroll told me they received instructions to replace the red ones. I didn't think we would be able to see them." The mosquito net was pulsing, one flash every second. We could sense it with our eyes closed as the strobe flashes reflected off the low cloud cover.

"Oh Kirby, what have they done?" I began to sob, letting loose an unrelenting tension.

"This will drive us insane!" his eyes were slits in an angry face. It was a nightmare we couldn't wake up from.

"I'll go talk to Carroll tomorrow and find out what we can do." We snuggled together shutting our eyes tightly, like children trying to keep the night monsters at bay.

Carroll was working as a technician at VOA. He had been our friend and mentor from the first day we arrived in Punta Gorda. We found him at home and asked, "Why did they switch to strobes?"

"It's some regulation out of Washington. It doesn't make much sense here since it is illegal to fly at night anyway. It seems a bit of overkill—the red lights should have been adequate. I'll see what I can find out."

We had intentionally not cleared our property; the surrounding forest and its creatures had always given us a feeling of security, as if we were participants in God's grand plan, but now our defenses had been breached. It was ironic that the people in town and even the guards in the compound, who were fully exposed to the lights, hardly noticed them. A pulsing night sky meant little when their whole environment was lit by yard and street lights. It was obvious that in seeking a natural environment where, among other things, it got dark at night, we were going against the flow—trying to turn the clock back. Two long weeks later we talked to Carroll. He explained, "There are a couple options that might improve the situation. The two arrays of towers have separate wiring. They can be set so they aren't all blinking at the same time as they are now. The strobes also have two settings for intensity: high for daylight use and low for nighttime. Presently they are set on high both day and night."

It was a blessing to have a friend on the "inside." Kirby wasted no time in going to talk to the station manager. It took several weeks before the approval to make both intensity and frequency changes was received from Washington, and shortly thereafter the changes were implemented. After weeks of "torture by strobe" it was a great relief. Meanwhile the perimeter lights had been turned to face outward, and now we had to pass through a third of a mile of floodlights and security cameras on our way home. Maintaining a neighborly relationship was going to be a trial. It seemed as if we would have to be forever vigilant to keep our turf from being invaded.

I have never had any difficulty expressing my emotions, but Kirby internalized stresses. The building project and the continuing tensions with VOA caused his nightly chest pains and frequent stomach aches to become more severe. Acceptance of this intrusion in our lives was more difficult than just saying the words.

We naively assumed we had, if we chose, the option to continue the life we had developed at Orange Point. Now a peaceful coexistence seemed impossible. From this new perspective the boat project, instead of being an exercise in creativity, skills development and a way to achieve a dream, became a means of escape from an intolerable situation. Our only choice was to keep focused on the tasks at hand; seeing the night sky without light pollution would come only after we launched the boat. We went back to work with more purpose than ever.

The night rains had stopped and the air was misty and cool as we started our hike in to meet the early bus with a six weeks' worth of KirbyKraft items on our backs. We left our muddy road, now well-lit with the floodlights and, thanks to VOA, we had a new concrete bridge to cross the creek instead of the old wooden one. The bus was half full of friendly souls as we turned inland at Cattle Landing a mile north of town. Every few miles we picked up parcels, messages to be delivered and people: Garifuna in Punta Gorda, East Indians in Forest Home and Mayas from the interior. We turned right onto the Southern Highway which runs along the foothills of the Maya Mountain range about ten miles inland from the swampy shoreline.

We passed Stone's, Whitney's, Genus' and Sellers' sawmills, all of which had supplied us with boat lumber, and on into the sparse vegetation of the pine ridge area. A few hours later we turned west on the scenic Hummingbird Highway, climbed through the citrus orchards of the fertile Stann Creek valley and crossed over the northern end of the mountain range. Refugees from El Salvador had recently settled in the highland areas and were growing and selling vegetables and producing powdered lime for the citrus industry.

In Belmopan we debussed at the market place where every color and shape was represented in the vendors and in their fruits and vegetables. Just beyond were the government administration offices. The capitol building itself was set on a higher level like an ancient Mayan temple.

Seeking another outlet, we met the manager of the new convention hotel who invited us to his home. Over tea his wife bought a good selection of craft items for her gift shop. We were off to a good start! It was always a challenge to make the shift from craftsman to salesman—Kirby likened it to putting on a tie. Though it didn't come naturally to either of us, it was an essential part of the business and, as in so many ways, we were most successful as a team.

Another bus, with standing room only, took us to Belize City and we arrived at Marin's guest house in late afternoon. We visited Robert and his wife, Linda, in the evening. He was rebuilding a 70-foot Chesapeake "buy boat" at a yard in the city. His tribulations with getting good labor and materials made our problems seem trivial; still he wouldn't compromise the quality of either. He was a power pack of energy and the project was moving along. It gave us heart.

Simeon Young was building a 25-foot mahogany sloop at the creek side and we took the opportunity to watch him work. It was always a marvel to see how fast a real professional worked. Later Kirby's comments were, "A professional knows how to make good joints but also, where he can get away with quick ones. We amateurs waste a lot of time trying to make them all perfect."

We visited Nick and Lou who had recently moved from Placencia. Loving their schooner, they had found a house to rent along the sea where *Miss Lou* could be moored close by. They had been carrying charter groups, and we were eager to hear about their experiences. Chartering seemed an attractive occupation—sail and get paid for it. But, like most ways of making a living, there were positive and negative aspects. Their smooth trips were offset by others with demanding and/or drunken guests, sudden squalls and seasickness.

During the next two days, we contacted six gift shop managers and sold all but three pieces. For a moment we had almost $2000 in the bank, but we knew the boat project would swallow it quickly.

The bus company was economizing; after three tire changes, we arrived home near midnight. Our friend Eleanor was waiting for us in something just short of panic. She motioned for us to come in through the back door; there were six unknown, Spanish-speaking people camped on the front patio. They had arrived after dark, and since the house was already closed up, she had decided to remain inside and avoid any confrontation. Considering our condition after our ten-hour bus ride, that seemed like a good solution. We put the dog inside, loaded the shotgun and went upstairs to bed. Too wired to sleep, I heard them leave in the wee hours.

Sometimes we do our clearest thinking in an exhausted state, as if all facades and emotional armor have been put aside, too heavy to bear. We had gone to the city to sell our crafts but, more importantly, for Kirby to get an EKG exam to determine the condition of his heart. His intermittent chest pains had continued and his blood pressure was very high, but when we arrived there the only cardiologist in the country was on holiday. On the way back from his closed office Kirby declared, "That's it! That's the sign. Even if an EKG had shown I have a problem, I wouldn't go for surgery—so what's the point; it would just give me something to worry about. I'm psyched out and it's time to get over it and try to heal myself."

A healthy diet and a positive frame of mind had been the essentials of my medical philosophy and applying it to my family had always worked, but to hear this spouted back to me from my science-minded husband was worth a chuckle. Not wanting to dampen his ardor, I decided not to state the obvious; having money in his pocket for the first time in months wasn't bad medicine either.

17

~~~

August 1986 to January 1987

AUDACITY AND ART

Almost by definition, creative projects require an element of audacity. Building a sailboat with very little money falls into this category, as well as a number of other categories that are even less complimentary. In Belize being audacious is not remarkable—audacity could be the national motto. If the state of New Hampshire, with the same land area, decided to become an independent country, with its own constitution, currency and government, it would still not approach Belize's audacity—New Hampshire has four times as many people and its borders are not under dispute. But, back on September 21, 1981, it happened; the United Nations recognized Belize as a sovereign and independent nation.

The move toward independence was complicated by Guatemala's historical claim to the territory and her threat to prevent Belize's independence by military intervention. The regional hegemony of the United States included Guatemala, and having Belize as a part of that larger nation would have been a simple solution. In addition, Britain was anxious to free herself from the financial drain of the colony and seemed willing to give up Belizean territory in return for Guatemala's blessing. But the

Belizean people stood firm on the issue, and Premier Price, over time, had adopted the stance of giving up "not one square centimeter." He successfully piloted Belize's ship of state through these murky waters to independence without giving up territory.

Belize had already been self-governing for 17 years and independence brought only a few immediate and obvious changes: the Union Jack was replaced by the new Belize flag, Premier Price became Prime Minister Price and he and his government continued to govern, their five-year term due to end in late 1984. But, the day after independence, Belize awoke to the rude realities of regional politics and international finance.

Belize had chosen to be non-aligned during the Cold War and wanted to maintain that status. By request the British army had stayed on to defend the country; the Price government was adamant about not having them replaced by American troops. The new nation was far from being financially self-sufficient and suddenly Britain was not there to guarantee the loans essential for operation. Belize had few choices. She could join the International Monetary Fund and seek financing through the World Bank and the Caribbean Basin Initiative, but, in doing so, she would give up much of her just-won freedom. The alternative was to request help from Cuba with whom she had maintained a friendly relationship. Grenada had done so and had suffered an invasion. Nicaragua also received Cuban help and was still being punished for it. As the lesser of evils, Belize joined the IMF and the winds of change were put in motion.

In June of 1983, the legislature passed laws that increased the taxes on all utilities, gasoline, beer, and soft drinks. The measure was made in an effort to raise $15 million and avoid currency devaluation. After an IMF evaluation, Belize was encouraged to provide a favorable climate for foreign investors and the traditional bar-stool schemers and dreamers were replaced by serious businessmen with capital. In the Toledo district large tracts of land were purchased by Americans for citrus, rice and cattle production. The first foreign-owned shrimp farm was built in central Belize, and several large American-owned resorts were built in the north. In May of 1984, $13 million was received to make payments on existing loans and to pay off overdue bills owed to U.S. businesses. Privatization of all government-run "authorities" was recommended. Education and medical budgets were to be reviewed. Efficiency in staffing government offices and the re-evaluation of teachers' salaries was suggested.

A new government was elected in December 1984 in a healthy, democratic election. The former opposition appeared undaunted as they walked into the maelstrom of change that had been initiated. At first these changes had little effect on the man in the street. Then influences entered that threatened the general populace more directly as Prime Minister Esquivel was persuaded to accept a portion of the refugees from the Central American conflicts. Salvadorans came, bringing with them little but a long history of war and violence, from a society that had lost sight of peaceful ways of settling problems. The international community provided programs to help these refugees, bringing aid and providing the kind of opportunities that many Belizeans had never had. Thus, there were tensions from the start. Tina overheard a conversation on the bus vehemently expressing the resentment of "born here" Belizeans.

"Cho maan, de gives 'em land, blocks for dehn house and seeds to plant. No give me none!"

"Have compassion, maan, dehn peoples come with not'ing, no land, no clothes, not'ing!"

"I no ask for plenty. Fu two years I been tryin' to get papers on one lee piece of land and not'ing yet!"

There were also more and more unofficial refugees from the ongoing civil war in Guatemala who slipped across the border and integrated into local communities, sometimes bringing intimidating ways and violent behavior. Although it never happened, the situation was complicated even further by leaders of Belize's Black community proposing to bring in Haitians to maintain the ethnic balance. The Belize we had known, a relatively harmonious place to live, was suddenly full of strife.

As significant as these changes were for the country, they had far less effect on individuals than did the introduction of television into the home. Satellite technology had arrived, and in every major municipality a company was established that picked up the satellite signal and rebroadcast it locally. For a monthly fee and the cost of the set, American culture, as packaged by TV producers, was introduced into homes around the country. The impact of foreign ways and values was immediate. Community sharing had kept a certain degree of equilibrium and most people accepted the hardships and did their best to enjoy life anyway. For the first time, Belizeans who had never been abroad compared their personal possessions with those seen in the programs and commercials and it brought home their status in the world.

The goal of commercial television is to sell products by making the viewer discontented with what he has. Belizeans were no less vulnerable than anyone else, but many lacked the means to purchase and therefore only reaped the discontent. The advent of television broke down the practice of socializing on front porches, under trees or at the seaside. Early on it was like a contagion and some businesses and government offices became non-functional during the time the soap operas were showing. But it was the glamorizing of violence that would prove to have the most devastating and long-lasting effect on the society.

We were concerned about these great winds of change moving through Belize. Unlike most Belizeans, we had had experience with the "buying bug" and knew what the long-range consequences of this new consumerism were likely to be. It wasn't going to be simply an increase in convenience, comfort, and entertainment; concurrently would be greater levels of borrowing that, if poorly managed, could lead to resource depletion and ultimately the loss of the freedom that had so recently been achieved. We feared that now that the door was open, the hurricane of "progress" would turn this peaceful little country upside down.

With tremendous odds against her survival as an independent nation, Belize was facing these daunting challenges, working with the skills she had, and giving the effort her all. We could do no better than to follow her example.

We had put the hull together with the best materials we had available and with the finest craftsmanship we were capable of. But art is an essential ingredient in every creative project; we strove to make her beautiful as well as strong.

A stout rub rail was run along the sheer to protect this vulnerable corner where the hull side joins the deck. It was made of straight-grained, black cabbage bark and was through-bolted. A toe rail, seen on many yachts, seemed inadequate and we decided to build a short bulwark with a rail cap. It was a far more complex project, but it was more versatile and it suited her workboat heritage.

Stanchion blocks were shaped to extend the curve of the hull-sides five inches above the deck, their outer edge leaning outboard to reflect the flare near the bow, straightening amidships and curving inboard near the stern, each stanchion varying slightly from its neighbors. The vertical bulwark plank wrapped around these stanchions and reflected the same gradual twist, until a few feet from the stern, where it was "rolled" to join the heart-shaped transom. The horizontal rail cap was also shaped to sweep around and cross over the transom. This cap and the corner pieces had to be carved from large blocks of wood since they were curved in both the horizontal and vertical planes.

It was complex work, and two months were spent on the effort, but we were extremely happy with the result. The rail was functional and added strength to the boat, but it was still fine enough to match the character of a lady. Pete Culler emphasized the importance of proportion in boat design and construction but admitted there were no definite rules. He concluded that if it *looked* right it was right. The curves had resolved themselves in a satisfactory way much as they had in the lofting process and in our eyes she looked good from every angle. It seemed extravagant to spend so much time on art when there was so much work remaining, but we seemed to have something guiding our hands, as if the creative aspect of the process had taken control.

The completed deck, now with a handsome rail around its outer edge, only covered about half the top surface of the boat; two large rectangular holes, one for each cabin, still remained open. A frame was built inside each opening with vertical members extending above the deck that served, like the hull molds had, as a form to bend the cabin side planks around. The line made by the upper edge of the cabin is almost as important as the sheer itself in its contribution to the overall look of the boat. Once again Tina perched on the stepladder some distance away. I adjusted the batten that would mark this line until I saw her signal of "perfect." We had the cheek to "improve" on the designer's line by running it more parallel with the sheer. It was a subtle change but more pleasing. We reckoned that Pete might have done the same if he hadn't needed to have a full six feet of head room.

Almost 18 inches high, the cabin sides used two strakes that came together with a splined joint. Rabbetted posts, made in two pieces, secured the corners. Edge boring the sides for the vertical bolts was the most challenging part of the job. The key was keeping a sharp bit and both eyes open when sighting.

Before the forward and aft cabin ends were fastened in place, "stopwaters" were inserted at the ends of each of the deck strip seams. Stopwaters are common looking dowels and don't get the credit they deserve. They are inserted in places where caulking alone cannot do the job of keeping the water out. Though they are usually out of sight in the finished product, they can make the difference between a wet boat and a dry one.

We, like many amateurs I'd read about, concentrated our resources on getting the hull built, figuring we would deal with finishing expenses when we came to them. Well, we came to them when we priced the eight ports we needed for the cabin sides. From the catalog these few pieces of

hardware would cost more than all the lumber we had put in the hull. There had to be an alternative.

Tina remembered that L. F. Herreshoff had used some simple ports in his *Golden Ball* design. A single plate of glass was set in a trough and the port was opened by removing the glass or by sliding it sideways. She saw another version of the moveable-plate-type port in a foundry catalog. The principle was simple, but the price in cast bronze was astronomical. I decided to combine the two concepts and make them out of wood.

The first step was to make a jig to router a flat rectangular area so the glass would fit snugly against the curved cabin side. More jig making, routering, doweling and some lathe work produced two round deadlights, four opening ports for the fore cabin and two for the aft. Since they swing inboard at the top they can be left open for ventilation in all but the heaviest rain storms. An eccentric at each end holds them closed. The channel below the lower edge drains out through the cabin side. The glass can be replaced with screens or with plywood shutters. I calculated I had made $2000 U.S. that week; of course saved money is hard to spend if you never had it in the first place.

18

~~~

January 1987 to November 1987

CRACKING UP!

The New Year rolled in, the fourth since we started lofting the boat. We were celebrating by having our morning coffee onboard. The air was cool and the sky clear, the effects of a cold front that had crossed over the day before. In our relaxed mood we took stock of our accomplishments and the tasks that lay before us.

The bulwark and cabin sides were in place; we weren't far from getting her closed up. Most of the big jobs had been completed, but the myriad of smaller ones still remaining were almost overwhelming. As we had put off facing the material costs of finishing the boat, so had we put off facing the time requirements. Cabin tops, companionways, hatches, interior joinery, spar building, rigging; the list went on and on. Lots of individual pieces, each requiring shaping, fastening and finishing, were connected to ever-increasingly expensive pieces of hardware and equipment. We still talked about fitting expenses into the budget, but in truth, financial planning had dropped by the wayside. Our budget was simple; we pushed the craftwork as hard as we could, we spent the earnings on boat materials and kept out just enough to continue working and eating.

On a much larger scale, the Belize government was in a similar situation. The most abundant resources, the logwood and mahogany, had been skimmed off during the first wave of colonialism. Belize's export earnings now came primarily from citrus, sugar, and marine products. With more exposure to the outside world, the Belizean people were becoming more dissatisfied with what they had and were asking more of the government. A rapid increase in private vehicles brought demands for better roads; villagers wanted electricity to operate their new televisions. Increased spending was the only choice the government had if it expected to see a second term, and this meant either borrowing more money or selling off assets.

Despite financial difficulties, Belize and the other countries of the region were trying to take charge of their own affairs. The Esquipulas Peace Accord, initiated by President Arias of Costa Rica, was signed by five Central American presidents. Among other things it called for democratization, free elections and "termination of all assistance to irregular forces," in obvious reference to the United States support of the Contra rebels. Belize's Foreign Minister Dean Barrow addressed the United Nations saying the Central American Peace Accord should not be interfered with by "outside powers that want to make Central America a political arena."

Below this laudable shouldering of responsibility and display of independence lay the fact that the United States remained the financial broker for the region, and when on "Black Monday" the stock market crashed, every nation shuddered. We shuddered too, not because we owned stocks, but because we recognized what a vulnerable situation we were in. Belize manufactured virtually nothing; she imported all her fuel (the only source of electricity), all building materials except wood, nearly all clothing and most of her food.

One of our goals in coming to Belize had been to achieve self-sufficiency and we had chosen a good place; both the

Maya and Garifuna cultures had, until recent times, subsisted on what the immediate environment would provide. Though we had moved a long way in that direction we had never arrived. We just couldn't give up buying new reading material and making a trip now and then; both books and travel required cash. Still we had reduced our material needs significantly—unless we counted the boat.

We had put all our financial resources toward her completion, but it was apparent that we wouldn't have the money to install the engine before we launched. That was a source of worry. But if the financial crisis continued and we had no fuel to operate the engine, what would be the point? Wasn't that one of the main reasons for building a wind-powered craft—another step toward simplification? It is so easy to lose sight of the goal!

So we put aside our engine worries and took what little cash we had to buy extra machetes and files, fish hooks and line, matches, rice and corn, soap, radio batteries and kerosene. Black Monday was the wake-up call we needed and we went back to work with reordered priorities and a renewed sense of purpose.

Beam shelves were glued in place along the cabin sides, and crowned beams were made by laminating seven layers of Santa Maria. The beams were finished with varnish, notched in and fastened. It would be unusual for a coastal boat to experience ocean waves breaking on these cabin tops but the laminated beams should hold up if that were to happen. Because we were now working well above the waterline where weight decreases stability, lighter materials were used when possible. Mahogany, one of the lightest woods we had available, was used for the cabin decking. The tongue and groove strakes were fitted, painted with cream-colored enamel, and fastened to the beams. Like everywhere else, the fastenings were counter sunk and either covered with wooden bungs or filled with epoxy/silica putty.

Having a watertight deck is essential for the longevity of a vessel and the comfort of the crew. A small leak below the water line does little to promote rot and unless it becomes severe can be taken care of with the occasional use of the bilge pump. However, a miniscule leak in the deck becomes a major issue if it happens to land on the face of a sleeping crew member, on electronic gear or on navigational charts. If it is fresh water and is trapped between wood surfaces it is likely to cause rot.

One of the joys of working with wood is the recognition that it was once a living thing—an organic material. Even after the tree is cut, wood retains life by swelling and contracting with relative humidity changes. (We learned to leave a little slack in the lids of our rosewood bowls to allow for the shrinkage that would inevitably occur in drier climates. Tina's sister, in Wisconsin, loved her sugar bowl but returned it for repair when the lid was too big to fit. By the time we received it back in Belize, the bowl had swelled again and there was no problem!) A properly-planked and caulked bottom will stay tight for many years as long as it is kept immersed. On the other hand, a deck is alternately wetted by spray and rain then dried by sun and wind. It is continually swelling and shrinking and requires special treatment to remain watertight.

We had built *Sunalee's* decks and covered them with canvas laid in roofing tar. The decks remained dry until the canvas was torn by the anchor. We knew our new boat would get some rough use freighting lumber and rosewood chunks, so we decided to break with tradition and employ the latest technology—a covering of Dynell cloth bedded in epoxy resin. It was very expensive, but according to the literature it was more flexible than the wood itself and was nearly bullet proof. Pete had always said, "The old ways work." We should have listened. (After launching, our wood started adjusting to the drier atmosphere away from the humid forest. Hairline cracks developed in our deck covering and we had to use elastomeric paint to reseal it.)

Pete gave a lot of useful information in his numerous articles, but he was criticized for the scarcity of detail he put in his plans. He expected the builder to know how to do it or be able to figure it out. John Burke, a close friend of his and a collector of his designs, said that Pete expected the builder's artistic talents to flower as the boatbuilding progressed. We believed our talents had bloomed when we built the bulwarks and lined out the cabin sheer, but for choosing the cabin details there was more adaptation involved than art.

We shortened the aft end of the main cabin by several inches. This change in framing allowed us to have a real walk-through (crouch-through) engine room with sliding doors in front of and behind the engine. The added space on deck would be used for deck boxes to house our butane bottles. Pete had designed the boat for use in New England; in the tropics space on deck is often more important than interior accommodations.

Good ventilation is also of high priority. A few degrees of temperature make a big difference in comfort level but keeping the air moving is even more important, for the welfare of the crew and also the boat itself. We launched *Sunalee* with the fore hatch opening forward to scoop in the breeze. We expected a blast of wind to sweep through the tiny cabin—it didn't. It wouldn't even blow out a candle. I pulled the hinge pins and set the hatch to one side, and voila, the candle was out, surprisingly, from a draft entering the companionway and moving forward through the cabin. I re-hinged the hatch to open aft, and our ventilation problem was solved. The natural flow was opposite to the wind direction, and the hatch acted more efficiently as a vent than a scoop. A side benefit was that with a dodger over the fore hatch and a tarp over the boom, the hatch and companionway could be left open in a rain shower.

The main cabin on the new boat would be well ventilated by using the same technique, but getting air flow through the aft cabin, without a hinged hatch, was more of a challenge. The opening in this smaller cabin was nearly as long as the cabin itself to allow passage for the engine. A low, removable doghouse was built that extended six inches past the opening. This forward part of the house was designed as a Dorade (vent); it allowed air to escape from the cabin through a four-inch opening in the house corner. Water was prevented by a baffle from entering the cabin and was drained out through scuppers.

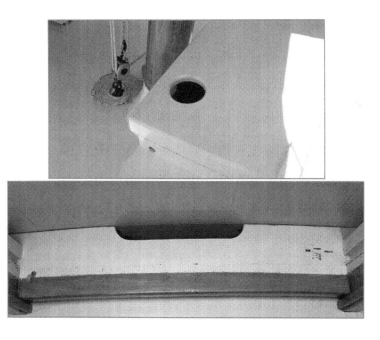

In our area a night rain of five inches is not unusual, and no matter what gasket material I used, one or more of the six hatches on our trimaran had always leaked. The moisture, heat, and stagnant air conspired to start rot in the hull compartments. Brand-name marine hatches were out of our financial reach but even they can leak in tropical downpours. Tina found the solution in a hatch design by the English yachtsman, Maurice Griffiths. His books were favorites of ours, and we related to his love of short-range cruising as well as his practical ideas.

Maurice was the editor of *Yachting Monthly* for forty years, wrote several cruising books, and designed a number of small, shallow-draft sailing boats. His leak-proof hatch was simple in principle and construction. A standard hinged cover with butt joints is constructed with dimensions four or five inches longer and wider than the cutout in the deck. Combings that are higher than the joint in the outer cover are then put in place around the opening. Water getting through the cover joint is blocked by the higher combings and drains out through small scuppers. We employed these principles in our fore hatch and both companionway slides. Standard washboards, slightly wider at the top for ease of use, were employed to close the aft end of the companionways. The top washboards were equipped with vent holes and a slide to close them off. Letting air in and keeping water out is the essence of cabin design in warm climates.

Though we were producing and selling more KirbyKraft items than ever, it seemed we were always broke, and the moments of exhaustion were becoming more frequent. At the end of a particularly big day, I suggested, "We could finish the cabins, charter her out and use the income for buying the time and materials to finish her later—we wouldn't have to launch. You have heard of bare-boat charters where you don't have a captain, well this would be a dry-boat charter where you don't have a sea. The ad could read, 'The sailboat, *Hyan Dreye*, is available for charter.' Our motto would be, 'Always steady as a rock.'"

"Guaranteed, no seasickness," Tina added, warming to the idea. "No finicky outboards and wet dingy rides—bike from boat to bar."

"No anchors to haul or drag; sleep the whole night through."

"Do you think we're cracking up?" she added after a moment.

"Probably, but I doubt anyone will notice."

With a little humor to cushion us from the hard edges of reality, we went back to work. *One step at a time, one step at a time*, had become our mantra. Don't waste your time fussing about the multitude of daunting tasks that lie ahead. Do you know how to do the next step? Okay, do it!

19
~~~

May 1987

MOTHER OR MATE

The arrival of our 22 year-old son was a welcome diversion from the intense concentration of the previous four years. Scott appeared on a dark, rainy night in November— exhausted and butt sore from a 3,000-mile, motorcycle journey from Montana. He had slept on roadside tables in drifting snow and in weigh stations. He made a brief stop in Dallas to see Christie and Carlos. He stayed in cheap hotels in Mexico where his motorcycle would be off the street but where the all-night traffic in the halls disturbed his sleep. He had graduated from college in the spring and had worked off some of his school debt on the family farm during the summer and fall. Now was the time to touch home base before he started a full-time job.

Christie and Carlos would be returning in the late spring to build their house, and we needed to get their construction materials trucked in when the road was dry. Combining that with lathe work and boatbuilding, we were swamped and were relieved when Scott took on many of the tasks. With machete and chainsaw, he cleared and stumped-out a roadway to their house site. On the lathe he turned rosewood bangles and sold them as he travelled about the country while trying to find a buyer for his motorcycle.

He scouted the job market and received an offer from a large sawmill/farming company. But when he sold his bike in early February, he was ready to go again. "Mom, I have been here long enough. This place is too confining for me right now. I need to go back to Montana and see what I can do there. Maybe I'll find my dream."

He had wanted to help us launch the boat but that was clearly not going to happen soon. We had enjoyed having him with us; his wry humor often saved the day. He was good help and resourceful in solving any problem that came up. But no, Belize didn't hold enough for him. He still hadn't found a direction for his life. It was another tearful parting, at least for me. But his return showed that we had not lost him entirely.

Belize had played, and was still playing, an important role in our lives. Our first years were crammed with new experiences that had given us a broader perspective of the world, and now our creative talents seemed to be blossoming in this tropical environment. Still, we couldn't expect it to offer the same to our children; they were at different stages in their lives and post-independent Belize was not the same place as British Honduras in 1972. We couldn't predict what role this little country would play in their futures.

Even though they had purchased the property adjoining ours, we were surprised when Christie and Carlos actually gave up their jobs in Texas to return home. They arrived in late May, rested a few days and then gathered a crew to begin digging foundations and a hole for the septic tank. Having spent every evening for the last year designing this structure they knew just what they needed to do and couldn't delay—the rains were imminent. Within six weeks the concrete walls had been cast and preparation for the roof structure had begun. Carlos was a man who knew how to work a crew and he accomplished a great deal in a short period of time. As Kirby said, "Carlos has got it in GO!"

"My, this is a good-sized house!" We were standing within the walls, surveying the work already done. "We want our house to be spacious and open where we can look out at the sea and the forest." While living in the manager's apartment of a storage complex in Dallas the only thing they could see outside their window was asphalt and concrete. Christie glowed with the satisfaction of making this plan become a reality.

Carlos' active mind had absorbed every detail of his construction experiences in Dallas and he had incorporated the concepts into his building techniques. They each had specific ideas about what this house should be and a vision of what the future would hold. They wanted a home to raise a family in. This was their dream and they were making it happen. In doing so, they were proving to be a good team.

Except for sharing the Point for brief periods of time with Scott and Ron, we had been alone for the better part of five years. It was an adjustment to have other permanent residents on the place, but they brought a fresh perspective. Scott had rallied round us, sharing our feelings about VOA's intrusion. But Christie's perception of the changes on Orange Point was different.

Dallas was an opportunity they were grateful for and because they knew how to live thriftily and work hard they had been able to build their nest egg in a short period of time. But as soon as they had enough savings to pay for the property and the building materials, they headed home. The area in Dallas where they had been living had grown into a mega-business district during the few years they were there, inundated by the construction of multi-storied buildings, malls, and suburban tracts. The increase in bad air, noise, and the ills of a larger population had affected her health and mental attitude. Orange Point represented real living and VOA was but a minor imperfection in their new landscape. More challenging for them would be learning to handle the cultural stresses in their new situation.

Our family unit was close, probably closer than most U.S. families because we had depended so much on each other in our new environment. But we each had our personal space, our own possessions and the liberty to perceive the world differently. Carlos had grown up with strong family bonds too, but with a greater feeling of equality among siblings. The good fortune of any member was expected to be shared among the others. There would be inevitable cultural and family tensions, but they had been married for more than six years, and their relationship seemed strong enough to survive.

For Kirby and I, coming to Belize had been an experiment; a year or two away from the States would give us a broader perspective—a chance to learn how people from other cultures lived. Fifteen years later the experiment continued—we were still learning. Our first lesson taught us there are many successful ways to deal with life's challenges. Christie and Carlos could choose the methods that would serve them best, just as we were trying to do.

Christie's arrival presented me with a new dilemma. I was proud of her choice to lead a healthier lifestyle than she could find in the city and her willingness to sacrifice many material things so she could be connected to Nature and to us. But I had not predicted her return to this rugged life on the Point, and in her absence Kirby and I had evolved our own dream, one that would leave her expectations of living as an extended family unit unfulfilled. And what of my own emotions as a mother who had just been reunited with her daughter and friend, one who had been far away for five years? Would I be able to sail away? It seemed like whatever I chose I would lose something precious. My conflicting emotions had me fighting depression.

It was time for me to employ the healing balm of hard work. Shop work was mandatory for we were indebted to Christie and Carlos for all the hardware and finishes they had brought for us. We had plenty of rosewood orders and boat work; it was just a matter of putting in the time. Although the work demanded a certain concentration, it allowed time for thought and would hopefully lead to a resolution.

During the next few months, the four of us established a bond based on mutual respect and trust. I grew confident that, having invested so much for so long, I needed to continue the journey I had chosen. Christie and I would find ways to support and nurture each other as we each continued to fulfill our dreams. Letting go of my conflicting emotions allowed me the energy to focus on the last phase of this building project while helping my daughter find equilibrium in her new situation . . . I recognized that, after all, I had always been both—mother and mate.

20
~~~

October--November 1987

PROVIDENCE

I climb up to the bow in the darkness of the boat shed—the sun is just beginning to paint the low-hanging clouds on the horizon a light pink. The glow fills me with momentary peace. Taking the ether of my dreams and giving it form has been a wondrous experience; that form is now a reality beneath me. My respite is brief.

This hull is huge compared to *Sunalee*—twice the draft and ten times the weight. *Sunalee's* shallowness allowed us to jump overboard and push her off when she grounded and even to haul her up on the beach for repairs. The raked keel and inside ballast of this new boat will be beneficial when grounding but there will be no pushing her off and a marine railway will be required to haul her for maintenance. All of this we knew when we chose her design; the real issue is the engine, which looms in the back of my mind like a dark shadow.

We sailed *Sunalee* to the other end of the country and back without an engine. It was a welcome challenge, giving us appreciation for the sailors of the freighting dories and fishing smacks before the advent of outboard engines. We got so we could handle her quite well under sail, but still we had to pole or paddle to get her into some of the tight upwind anchorages. Eventually Kirby installed a five-horsepower Briggs and Stratton to help the "lee fat gal" over the waves and through the currents of the main channel—both working against us as we made our way north. Though we have told ourselves otherwise, we both know the new boat needs an engine too, but it will take another year at the lathe to be able to finance all the paraphernalia necessary to install it.

We are feeling the press of time. The boat is sitting 75 yards from the water's edge and she must be moved when the ground is dry. We have six months before the rains will get heavy again. Where will the energy and resources come for this final push? We are both worn down to bone—so close and yet so far from seeing this boat in the water. I shake my head—I don't know how we will resolve these issues.

I remind myself that it is another new day—one that has the potential for making another step toward our goal. It is time to begin. I climb down the scaffolding, pat the hull, salute the rising sun, and go to make pancakes. Faith! Don't let me lose it now when I need it the most.

Kirby shifted from the relatively light-weight mahogany used in the cabin tops, to dense cabbage bark to build the rudder. He calculated the weight of the upper portion would neutralize the buoyancy of the part below water and reduce the wear on the rudder hinges. It is a substantial unit—ten feet long with the blade two inches thick and twenty inches at its widest point. After his experience fighting the tiller of the *Here and Now*, he decided to build in a trim tab, a rudder to steer the rudder, that would help offset any steering imbalance. He designed it to allow the top of the control shaft to end at the rudder's pivot point, so the tab could be used in conjunction with a self-steering vane. The plank joints were positioned so the channel for the half-inch control rod could be routered into the plank edge prior to assembly.

The rudder head extends above the transom cap where a socket allows the use of a standard tiller. Thirty inches below is another socket where a stub tiller can be inserted through a slot in the transom. This tiller would be below the aft deck and could be coupled to a drum and cable system for wheel steering.

Three pairs of gudgeons were fabricated by bending 1/8 by 3-inch stainless steel straps in a "U" shape and through-bolting one of each pair to the rudder and the other to the transom and sternpost. Blocks of lignum vitae were shaped and inserted into the "U"s of each gudgeon and doweled into place. Undersized holes were carefully positioned in each and using a homemade cutter on a long ½ inch rod the gudgeon holes were line-bored using a drill. The ¾-inch stainless steel rudder pin slid snuggly into place. To reduce turbulence the stem post was tapered and the forward edge of the blade was routered out to house the hinge pin; the rudder's after-edge was also tapered.

The result was a strong, functional and serviceable hinge system. With planning, ingenuity, careful craftsmanship and a lot of labor, we had managed to work with the materials we had available. We were really pleased.

Down below, the cabins had been made usable; I had places to store my supplies, a counter for my little stove, a gimbaled kerosene lamp, bunks for four people and a head. Work on the "temporary" shelves and bunks would be classified as carpentry, rather than cabinetry, but the permanent components—the splined forward bulkhead with its mahogany spindles at the top—had been built with strength and beauty in mind, as the companionway ladders would be.

The top step of the main cabin ladder is the same twenty-four inch width as the sill and the sides follow the tapered lines of the companionway opening so its lower step is only 16 inches wide. It not only looks right, its narrow base gives more leg room to crew seated on the settees. Each rung was fitted into a compound dado in the side pieces. I have a passion for dolphins and Kirby carved the upper hand grips in their shape. The black, cross-hatched, oval-tread pads of carbon wood contrast nicely with the varnished mahogany of the rungs and sides.

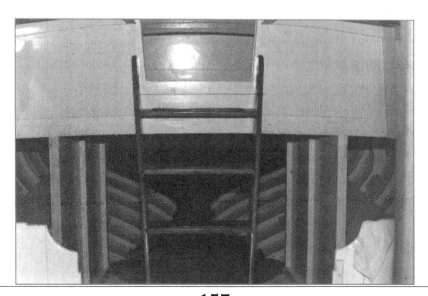

The aft cabin ladder was more complex since it would also be used as a boarding ladder. It was built with wide straight sides, the back portion having a set of narrow fixed steps. A channel was routered into the forward portion of the sides to accept a small ladder unit which can be slid up and down, much like a carpenter's extension ladder. Turned, wooden pins hold it in the up or down position. The top was designed to hang either on the cap rail or on a shelf inside the companionway. Large, turned pins hold it in position in either place.

Kirby gets his greatest satisfaction out of the projects that require original thinking. We had lovely dense hardwoods to work with and he enjoyed the challenge of substituting wood for metal wherever possible but even the densest timber would not do for making the anchor windlass. This is an essential piece of equipment for a coastal boat. Not only is it used for raising anchor, it can also be used to kedge a boat into deeper water after a grounding. Ron had a knack for sniffing out "good old stuff" and he found a gem of a windlass in a Miami River salvage yard. It was heavy enough to use for an anchor itself but compact and fit neatly between the foremast and the cabin. Kirby took it apart for servicing and was pleased with its ruggedness and simplicity. It had been built before the present era of planned obsolescence—it was patented in May 1915.

Just forward of the mast are the bitts. The bases of this pair of 5 by 5-inch cabbage bark posts are bolted to the fore knee; their heads protrude 15 inches above the deck. They are used to secure the anchor lines and also the inboard end of the bowsprit. As the vertical masts under tension are pushing on the bottom of the boat, the horizontal bowsprit is thrusting aft against the bitts.

The bowsprit itself was shaped from a 6 by 6-inch beam of Santa Maria twelve feet long. Three feet forward a mortise was cut in its lower face to accept the tenon of the stem timber. Metal clamps, the gammon irons, were installed on the stem faces to hold the sprit in position. The outboard eight feet were carved to an octagonal shape with the tip shouldered and squared for a stainless steel collar.

As the vessel began to have form and essence, people were attracted to her like bees to honey—the more form she took on, the more people came to visit until entertaining became an everyday occurrence. Many bought craft items and we certainly needed the income, but entertaining guests was enervating and when we were tired or feeling pressed for time, we didn't enjoy it.

The visits of Jed and Sarah were exceptions. They were longtime friends whose moral support and input we depended on. Jed was intensely interested in the project. Being a woodworker he understood the challenging nature of wooden boat construction and his compliments meant a lot. He would offer an opinion here and there on ways to solve problems, but he never interfered with the creative process that he knew was so keenly personal.

They lived nearby and came often to keep track of our progress. Jed had seen other boats being built and was aware that our time frame was unrealistic; after all, he had often seen us push it forward. He recognized this as part of the procedure and only rarely made an issue of our naiveté. Sarah was forthright in saying she did not understand what captivated us; sailing vessels did not speak to her in the same way. With time she caught a bit of the fever too and encouraged us to keep the faith. I think she understood that we had to do this or our lives wouldn't be complete.

In mid-October they came to survey the project and Kirby was showing Jed the nearly-finished rudder. "It looks like you're almost ready to launch. I see you went ahead with the trim tab. How did you bore for the shaft?" They turned to view the jig Kirby had made for long-line boring.

Sarah rubbed her hand along the curve of the transom cap, "It all blends in so beautifully. When will you hang the rudder?"

"Not until she is out of the shed and down by the shore." I hesitated, "We are anxious to launch her but there is no way we can earn the money for the rest of the gear and still get her in before the rains. We are sort of between a rock and a hard place."

Sarah looked dismayed. Jed listened and nodded, "You already have the engine; it's a shame not to put it in."

Kirby joined in, "That's true. I knew I would need some accessories but they add up to more than I paid for the engine: motor mounts, coupling, shaft, propeller, stern tube, marine manifold, fuel filters and tank and the list goes on. We are close enough to finishing the work; it's buying all that equipment that's the killer. Then there is all the ground tackle: anchor, lines, and chain. All of that must come before the engine."

"The truth of the matter," Jed said, "is that I could see this coming. Sarah and I talked it over and have a proposal to make."

"I'm listening," Kirby glanced at me.

"We are hoping to build a new house and could use some help. What do you think of a cash advance on your labor with the plan to start work a year from now?"

While we absorbed the impact of this offer, time seemed to stop; the birds sang, the waves lapped on the shore, and the wind rustled the leaves on the trees. "I must say it sounds pretty attractive." Kirby turned to put his arm around me; just the possibility of a way out of this dilemma took a huge weight off our shoulders.

Friends who go the extra mile are rare. We went into the house for coffee and cake to talk about the details. This had to be a clearly-understood arrangement or it wouldn't be worth it. We had seen too many friendships founder on the rocks of ambiguous business deals and we didn't want to risk that happening with the four of us.

This would be the first time we had gone into significant debt for many years, so when we were finally alone Kirby couldn't help but comment to me that he felt like he would be selling himself into servitude. But Jed did need help, and it was the opportunity we needed. Kirby joked, "I thought indenture had something to do with wearing false teeth."

Jed knew as well as we did that sitting another year in the damp forest environment would not do this vessel any good. She needed to be in her element as soon as possible. The old boat builder, Amigo, had commented some time ago that he feared we would have dry-rot and termites in the hull before she ever hit the water.

A week later, Kirby signed an agreement with Jed and went to the bank with a sizable check. Now we could concentrate on ordering the last bits of hardware and gear that every sailing vessel must have, as well as the engine accessories. We set about it with relief, earnestness and a fair amount of joy.

21

~~~

October 1987 to March 1988

IN THE EYES OF THE BEHOLDER

The whop, whop, whopping sound kept getting louder, and I put down my plane and went out to investigate. A helicopter, with British army markings, was setting down in our little clearing. The wash from the blades was blowing the thatch off our goat barn and the big machine was about to squat on our newly-planted cherry bushes. I rushed out, waving it off, until it rose again and slid toward the VOA clearing. Fifteen minutes later a British colonel arrived on foot apologizing for his transgression. He had been out on an early morning flight from the nearby camp and thought he would just stop in and see if his snuff box was finished.

The British army officers had been steady customers since we first started KirbyKraft ten years before. A regimental changeover occurred every six months, and each new group of officers presented us with new orders and new challenges; we had learned how to make inlaid backgammon boards, beer steins, and round picture frames; the present group wanted snuff boxes. Without hinges and hasps, I had worked out a technique to make a small disc-shaped bowl with a slightly oval lip and lid; a twist locked the lid in place so it could be carried in a pocket. A few orders were notable because the officer had "connections," and we had done gifts intended for members of the royal family, but this was the first time anyone had attempted to pick up an order by helicopter.

With the loan funds available to pay for the remaining equipment and material, I could limit my daily lathe work to two or three hours—just enough to cover our living expenses. The excuse for the slow progress on the boat was gone once we acquired the loan. The challenge now was to sustain the level of concentration necessary to finish the job.

We liked the looks of the quarter rail that Pete had drawn for his bigger schooners, and on Nick's *Miss Lou,* we had been able to see its functionality firsthand. On a boat as small as ours, adding such a structure could detract rather than enhance her overall appearance. It would be easy to overbuild, so we planned carefully and trusted our sense of proportion.

The top rails were run parallel to the sweep of the sheer but were extended four feet past the transom to be used as davits for lifting and carrying a dinghy. They were sawn out of two-inch stock in a curve which followed the deck line and continued the tumblehome displayed by the bulwarks. The rails were clamped into position, and large laminated knees were fabricated and fitted to the transom to support the extended rail. Spindles, each one cut to a different complex angle, were inserted every foot between the rails and the bulwark cap and through-bolted. The aft ends of the rails were slotted for sheaves and held together by a cross member having the same arc as the transom cap. Just above the cap itself, a similar cross member that would be used as a sheet traveler was notched in. Ogees completed the forward rail ends.

Though complex to build, it served several purposes: it would give more security to the cockpit crew, would serve as a traveler, and as davits. To our eyes we got the proportions right; it drew out and enhanced the sheer line and added to our *little ship* motif. Beauty, rather than being minimized by simplicity, was enhanced.

For this design, Pete had been commissioned to draw "the ideal small cruising boat," and one of its more unusual features was the sail configuration; we thought of it as the *Meadow Lark* rig because it was similar to the sail plan of L. F. Herrschoff's design with that name. Unlike the conventional ketch, both mizzen and main sails were almost identical in size and shape, and each was headed by unusually short gaffs. In theory, this rig should have the efficiency of the triangular Marconi sail but without the requirement for tall masts and their complex stays. It should also have the off-wind superiority of the gaff sail without requiring a two-part halyard system. The well-raked masts needed only a single shroud on each side and no back stays. The main and mizzen sails, a little over 200 square feet each, should be easy to handle. Two identical staysails, for light air sailing, are set flying (with only their corners fastened) and would be uncomplicated to raise and lower.

In our area we commonly experience a daily offshore/onshore wind pattern and do a lot of light-air sailing. Since her sail area/displacement ratio was fairly low, we were concerned that she would be under-canvassed. John Burke, Pete's protégé, assured us that this was an easily-driven hull and the designed sail plan should be adequate. We hoped he was right for we knew what it was like to drift around waiting for enough wind to get steerage.

Not long after we heard from Mr. Burke, I had unrolled our dog-eared plans and found that, in pencil, a topmast had been added to the mizzen. Attached was a note from Tina, "Why not a schooner! Doesn't it look great?" This was a simple solution for increasing sail area without changing the basic plan; just add a small, removable mast from which a big triangular staysail or a four-sided fisherman could be flown in light air. Purists would assert that it takes more than a topmast to make a ketch into a schooner, but none were around to chastise us. So it was that our main mast was renamed the fore, the mizzen became the main, and the so- called "no-bull ketch" morphed into the "no-bull schooner." I had been building a schooner all this time and didn't know it. Schooner! I liked the sound of it.

Every step of the boat work had been challenging to plan and to accomplish, and each had been satisfying when it was completed, but building the masts added a new element—excitement. Just the fact that the time had finally come to build them meant we were getting close to finishing the project. Their magnitude alone was impressive—each was as long as the boat itself.

Magnitude translates into weight, and having too much weight up high in a boat means instability. In continuing the theme of simplicity, Pete probably would have recommended the masts to be built from the solid trunk of some lightweight East Coast timber. Here in the tropics we have woods like Spanish cedar that are light but not strong and woods like Santa Maria that are strong but are not light. We decided to build with Santa Maria but to make the masts hollow. It would be harder, but it would reduce their weight by more than a third.

From a formula for making parabolic curves, I drew up a plan where the mast would taper from a seven-inch diameter at the boom to six inches where the gaff would ride and on to five inches at the mast head. We used a simple four-stave box construction, and both masts were built using the same techniques. The scarfs in the two-inch stock were staggered so no weak points were introduced. The side pieces were joined to give a pair of 34-foot staves. To keep them straight, they were pared down carefully by ripping off only thin strips and allowing for the spring of the wood. The two pieces were clamped together to make sure they would be identical and finished with a hand jointer. These pieces would dictate the fore and aft shape of the finished spar, and all the tapering was worked into the forward edge. The after edge was kept straight with the exception of the top five-foot section which was curved aft an extra inch. The idea was that the forward pull of the forestay would straighten it when fully rigged.

It was intended that the walls of the finished round mast would be uniform so the inside surface of each stave was coved out to a 2 to 2 ½-inch radius. This was done by using a small blade on a circular saw and making cuts every inch across or diagonal to the grain. The bulk of the wood was chipped out with mallet and gouge. A jig was made for the circular saw that allowed it to be pushed down the length of the stave in a diagonal position, thereby cleaning the cove out smoothly. The lower seven feet and the upper four feet were made solid by gluing a spacer block between the side staves. Wedges were cut out of the upper eighteen inches of the lower block that resulted in fingers that would prevent a hard spot, a weakness, from occurring when the mast bent under load.

The staves that made up the forward and after faces of the box were lined out with the taper evenly shared between its sides. They were coved out in the same way as the side staves, and the scarfs were cut and fitted. Clamps were made by building a box frame of 1 by 2-inch strips; three corners were fastened by screws and the fourth by a locking notch. A pair of wedges provided pressure. They were simple to make, inexpensive, and quicker to use than screw clamps. One at a time we glued the stave sections to the mast assembly. By not trying to glue the full-length stave, we minimized the number of clamps required and avoided the frantic race against the working time of our epoxy glue. (We thank Larry Pardey for that idea.) The end grain was sealed with epoxy resin and the remaining inside surfaces with several coats of Tina's pine tar/turpentine brew. Small air vents were bored, an electric wire was run, and the after-face stave pieces were glued in place to complete the box.

The rounding of a spar is a rewarding experience; it makes the simple scarfs appear complex, and the craftsman gets more compliments than he is due. But he accepts them gracefully, being fully aware of all the really hard things he has done that are never seen. Rounding a spar does require careful organization. The box structure was trimmed until it was exactly square in cross section. A marking gauge, described by Bud McIntosh in a *WoodenBoat* article, was used, the corners of the box were cut off at 45 degrees with a circular saw, and the whole spar was planed to a perfect octagon in cross section. The procedure was continued: sixteen sides, thirty-two, and finally the ridges lightly planed to approximate sixty-four. An electric plane was employed for roughing out with the final shaping done with the hand jointer. The goal was to maintain smoothness in the lengthwise direction and to avoid irregularity in the cross sections.

Bud also told how to make a simple drill-powered, belt sander which worked extremely well. Final sanding was done by hand, and several coats of clear, linear-polyurethane varnish were applied. The masts were beautiful; they came out far better than I would have expected considering the interlocking, wavy grain of the wood. As impressive as they were just lying on the shop floor, I could hardly wait to see them stepped in their vertical position.

After applying the last coat, I wandered back behind the shop where my brother was operating the "Falcon Forest Foundry." It was mid-February and to us the weather had been cool—in the low seventies at night and the low eighties during the day. But when Russ left his Montana ranch, it had been minus fifteen. Though uncomplaining, his sweat-drenched clothes indicated he was having trouble adjusting to the hundred-degree change. To make matters worse, he was tending a roaring fire of resinous pine scraps under a pot of molten lead. The lead was being ladled into molds to produce triangular ballast bars to fit between the floor timbers in the bilge.

In the States he had collected lead-coated cable and wheel weights that we had brought down in our last trip with the old bus. In fairness, I explained to him, he should be allowed to experience this process from beginning to end.

I had sent him drawings of the many pieces of complex hardware we needed to rig the boat, and he had painstakingly fabricated them from steel. Carlos had them galvanized in Dallas and brought them down. Some, like the spectacle irons for mounting the topmast, were truly art pieces. "When you finish this pour," I said, "I have another job that is even more exciting."

"Okay, I think I can tear myself away."

I loaded a six-foot piece of iron strap and a piece of channel iron half as long into the canoe, and we paddled into town and hiked back to the high school. I had rented their welding equipment, and Russ went to work fabricating the keel shoe. Metal was his medium and he worked it as a master; his torch cuts were smooth and straight and his welding was like a good caulking bead. "It must be a relief to get away from that hot wood fire," I commented as the sparks flew.

"I've been thinking how nice it would be to jump into a snowdrift," he said.

The shoe fit so we put it on; it extended six inches beyond the stern post. It protected the vulnerable joint between the post and rudder, and after through-bolting, the vertical straps reinforced the bond between the post and keel.

A few days later Russ was on his way back north to the welcoming snow drifts. From the beginning he had participated in our Belizean experience. Twice he had provided summer employment when I needed it badly and on his visits he always took part in whatever projects we had going. He enjoys travel and most of his trips contain an element of adventure, but snow, hail, flood or drought, Montana is his home.

22

~~~

January to March 1988

MIRACLES WITHOUT END

With the masts finished, we felt we were in the final stretch, running neck and neck with the rainy season. If it arrived at the finish line before we did, our track to the sea would become a bog, and we could plan on waiting another nine months before we could launch. There were a daunting number of tasks to accomplish during this final push, and we committed ourselves to efficiency and perseverance.

Engine parts were ordered from Perkins in England, a propeller shaft from Anchor Marine in Belize City and a friend was bringing an order from Jamestown Distributors in Rhode Island. We had ordered so many boat supplies from this marine dealer during the building process that a friendship had developed. On the outside of one shipping carton was a hand-written note: "Glad you are finally painting. When can I come for a ride?" Dave. We had put in a sawmill order for the big beams to make the launching cradle, and we expected everything to arrive soon, but we were still stumped on finding several critical items.

We had to have ground tackle before we could launch. We had our hearts set on a pair of Paul Luke's or their equivalent. We had figured a 40-pounder for daily use and one of about 75 pounds for a storm anchor. Pete recommended good anchor gear as the best kind of insurance. Luke's were made in Canada and would have to be sent by sea freight; even if they were in stock, the shipping might take months. At this time they seemed like a fantasy. We would have to look in the City for what was locally available.

Kirby was almost ready to set the engine in, but he still didn't have a propeller or a stern tube. He had seen boats with worm damage in the shaft alleyway that was almost impossible to repair—damage that would have been avoided with a properly installed tube. He had gone through the formulas in all his books and contacted two different manufacturers to determine the correct propeller for the Perkins. It would need to be eighteen or nineteen inches in diameter with a 12 to 14 pitch and turn right-handed. The manufacturer's prices were astronomical and even after getting the loan he couldn't make himself spend the money for a new one. He looked for a used one in Belize City without any luck.

Even while going back and forth to town making telephone calls and sending off money orders, Kirby managed to keep the boat construction going as well as doing his daily quota of lathe work. He hardened up all the caulking and I followed behind with putty for the seams. He built the topmast, the booms and gaffs from solid mahogany and rounded them in the same way he had the masts. He shaped and bored lignum vitae deadeyes for the shroud ends and faired the aperture to facilitate the smooth flow of water to the propeller.

One day Pedro stopped by with a fish for us and to look over the project. During their conversation Kirby explained the immediate need for twine; three days later Pedro came by with eight spools he had found in Guatemala. For months the fishing cooperative in Belize City had been out of this item. Now I could begin to learn the sailor's ancient skill of parceling and serving.

For centuries this method was used to protect the shrouds on sailing vessels and while it has a practical purpose, it is also a mark of authenticity for a traditional vessel, especially a schooner. The concept is to put a waterproof sheath over rope or metal wire that would otherwise deteriorate from exposure to the elements. Our shrouds were made up of seven solid strands of aluminum-coated steel wire. Over time the coating would disappear, and exposure to salt water would cause the steel to rust and weaken. With proper application and maintenance, parceled and served wire has been known to last for decades.

Traditional parceling was done by wrapping pine tar-soaked strips of canvas spirally with the lay of the wire or rope with edges overlapping to prevent moisture from entering. We substituted cloth friction tape for the canvas strips but applied it the same way after first coating the wire with pine tar.

The old time sailors served by covering the parceling with tightly-wound turns of marline against the lay. We used small diameter, number 21, nylon twine. Kirby made a serving mallet from a sketch in Hervey Garret Smith's extremely useful book, *The Arts of the Sailor*. The end of the mallet-shaped device contains a roll of twine. The shroud to be served is tightened, in our case between two trees, and several turns of the mallet are made to get the correct tension on the serving twine. By swinging the wire in jump rope fashion the mallet propels itself along and a fifty foot shroud can be served in less than an hour. It is tricky to get started and once going it is best not to stop. When the serving is complete the cable takes on a hard, smooth and attractive surface; the excess pine tar is wiped off and allowed to dry a few days and then given several coats of white enamel

The specially manufactured eyes that came with the cable were attached to the ends, seized to hold a thimble and were hand wrapped and served. It was a tedious job but one I had settled into.

It was early morning when I heard the dog's people bark as I worked at the third eye in a series of six. "No, no, not now," I grumbled to myself. "There is so much yet to do before we are ready to launch." Kirby climbed down from the boat to greet our unwelcome visitors. "Please head them off if you can." I whispered as he passed me.

"Morning, Minister," then I heard the murmur of introductions.

"Morning, Mrs. Esquivel. I am happy to meet you and your children. Welcome to Orange Point." Kirby's voice carried, telling me that we couldn't avoid this one. More introductions were too low to hear. Realization washed over me, *Good heavens! Mr. Wagner has brought the Prime Minister's wife and children.*

Kirby guided them into the boat shed, introducing me as he approached, "This is my wife, Tina."

"Morning, Mr. Wagner. Morning, Mrs. Esquivel . . . children. I hope you are having a good time in Punta Gorda. Sorry I can't shake hands right now." My arms were coated up to the elbows with sticky black pine tar.

"Yes, it is a pretty little town. We came in on the early flight for a meeting my husband has to attend, and poor Mr. Wagner has the task of entertaining us. But we can't find any place open for breakfast."

"Ahhh yes, P.G. is not long on breakfast places." I glanced at the minister, wondering, *No breakfast?*

Kirby waited for my cue while the minister looked anxious. Suddenly I was aware of their expectations. Internally I turned belligerent and told myself, *I am a working woman; I can't be on call to cook at the drop of a hat, even for the Prime Minister's wife!*

The children looked grumpy and out of sorts. I ignored my irritation at my own reaction and the presumed expectation and turned to Kirby, "Why don't you give everyone a tour of the boat project? I will try to finish up here quickly." He ushered them around the other side of the boat. I wrapped the last of the line and tied it off, glancing regretfully at the eyes yet to be done.

It took some doing to get my hands clean, but finally I tucked my ragged, streaked shirt into my jeans, tucked the jeans into my rubber boats, straightened my askew scarf and went to join the Prime Minister's wife with the faint hope that sympathy would substitute for sustenance. There was nothing in my pantry—no eggs, no flour. We had eaten the last of the bread and beans last evening. My sink was full of two days of dirty dishes. I had been caught totally off guard.

After our guests had left—still hungry—I went back to my work. While my hands were busy I reflected on my change of identity. To maintain a high degree of commitment to this project, I had had to give up on the image of myself as superwoman—capable of doing everything, including serving guests tea and cake.

My mother had a hard time believing how I had changed. As a young woman, I was fashion conscious and loved to dress well. For the first few months of marriage, I wouldn't let Kirby get out of bed until I had my "face" on and my hair styled. I was a good cook and strove for perfection in my housekeeping. I had been raised with a strict code of hospitality. In becoming an adventurer, I had taken a step in reordering my priorities, and now this creative process had carried me beyond the confines I had been taught as appropriate. Circumstance was helping me to be true to the choice I had made.

One afternoon Kirby came back from town smiling ear to ear. "You are not going to believe this! Our Jamestown order came; they didn't charge any duty." This news did not justify Kirby's goofy grin, but I recognized he was relating things as they happened and he would eventually get to the heart of the matter.

"Remember Julio had a Perkins in the *Rebecca* before he put in the big Ford? Well, he still had the old stern tube and it is exactly what I've been looking for. It's a little long but it will be easy to shorten and rethread. Then he remembered he had the old prop, too. He dug through his stuff and found it. It's a little beat up, but it is 18 inch, three-bladed with a 14 pitch, right-hand turning and it fits a 1 1/4 inch shaft. Can you believe it, right here in P.G.?"

Two weeks later we were in Belize City. We had taken the newly-arrived shaft, the coupling and the stern tube in for machining. Nick had sold us a small fuel tank which fit neatly under the cockpit and we were celebrating with dinner at their house. Lou asked, "What are you going to do about anchors?"

"Hofius has some big fishermen which are good out on the reef," Kirby replied. "The price is right but they aren't the greatest for our soft mud anchorages down south."

"I wonder if Jim still has his anchors," Nick said, "I don't think he sold them with the boat. I could give him a call." Jim and his wife Laura, who lived nearby, had built a lovely Crocker-designed sloop in their backyard.

The next day Jim led us down to his storage room. "The buyer didn't think he needed this heavy ground tackle, so I kept it." He flipped on the light, moved a couple of bikes and there they were—two Paul Luke anchors—a 40 and a 75 pounder. I felt goose bumps. Even Kirby was speechless. "I also have a spool of 5/8 line that is hardly used. You can have it all for what I have in it." Late that afternoon we sat stunned in our bus seats, trying to absorb all that had so quickly occurred.

Finding in Belize and purchasing the exact anchors that we had dreamed about was only the most recent in a series of amazing events. So many times there had been *just enough* material, without an inch to spare—starting with the keel timber and continuing with the planking, the cabin trunk and the rudder. At first we thought of them as lucky coincidences that were mostly due to our careful planning; later, as such events continued to occur, we had to admit there was something happening that was beyond our understanding. As we neared the completion of the project, these incidences were coming like an avalanche and we had given up trying to find reason in them; Ron's windlass fit perfectly, Jim and Gae had brought hardware that matched the spar diameters, Nick's fuel tank fit into the only space available for it, a steering drum Dale had on hand was perfect for the job, and Julio's propeller was right in pitch, diameter, shaft size and rotation—and now Jim's anchors. It was awe-inspiring to be on the receiving end of such phenomena.

During the course of the project we had learned a lot about harnessing the creative aspects of our minds and employing them to solve the puzzles that we continually faced. At the same time we had been training our hands to put those creative thoughts into solid form. We were familiar with that feeling of ecstasy when mind and hands were fully harmonized and our work was flowing; we had also experienced the doldrums when this coordination was broken and nothing seemed to go right. We had become aware of the nature of the environment required for us to work creatively, and we had each developed our own personal recipes for achieving and sustaining those conditions. All well and good, but none of these insights explained this rash of extraordinary events that made us feel we had a guardian angel.

It finally dawned on me that I was attempting to answer a question that people have been pondering since the dawn of history: what is the nature of this unknown element that powers the creative impulse of the universe? With the last of my day's quota of philosophical energy, I concluded that when one's body, creative mind and this mystical force are all in synchrony, miracles happen.

23

~~~

April-May 1988

EMERGENCE

Afternoon thunderheads indicated the dry season was coming to an end; we *had* to get the boat moved to the water's edge. We tried to think positively, that this pressure was an additional source of energy that would move us faster toward our goal. Carlos was pushing hard on dry season projects too, but came over to give me a hand setting the engine in place. He was sensitive to my inability to talk and work at the same time and knew whether his presence was a help or a hindrance.

I had built heavy engine beds of Bethabara and notched and drifted them into the floor timbers. I cut and folded a large sheet of lead into a full-length drip pan and sealed the corners with Dynel cloth and epoxy resin. A line-boring apparatus was set up to enlarge the ends of the shaft alley to accept the stuffing box and stern bearing housings, and a hole was bored in the stern post to allow for the insertion and removal of the propeller shaft. After assembly, waterproof grease was pumped in to fill the void between the stern tube and the alley itself.

A set of motor mounts and a water-jacketed exhaust manifold arrived from the Perkins dealership, and the original hot manifold was replaced. Through-hull fittings with sea cocks were installed amidships for the cooling water and exhaust ports. The huge flywheel, the secret to its ability to hand start, made the little engine a heavy brute. Removing the marine gearbox lightened it and made it easier to handle. I built a box around the engine base to provide a flat bottom surface. Carlos rigged a cable puller, beams, rollers, and safety lines for the lifting process, and we were ready to set the engine in.

With a couple of truck tires as safety cushions, he hoisted the engine up from the shop floor to deck level, and I slid a big beam under it. When prying it into position, it cleared the roof beam by a scant half inch. I sent a prayer of thanks to the boatbuilding angel looking after us—who knows, it may have been Pete himself!

Carlos laid two beams in a fore and aft direction on the roof joists using long 5/8 bolts as rollers between them. In hoisting the motor again, the cable puller transferred the weight to the upper beam. Turning the bolt heads with a ratchet moved the beam slowly forward carrying the engine with it. When in position it was lowered to the aft cabin sole. A short plank and rollers brought it over the engine bed amidships. Through a temporary hole in the deck, the cable puller lifted the engine into place on its mounts.

It seemed like half of our many visitors asked the question, "How will you get it in the water?" It was a reasonable query; as the toucan flies, the boat was only forty yards from the water's edge, but at that point, the bank was a sheer five-foot drop to the sea. Since I didn't know for sure how we would launch, I started asking for suggestions and over several years I heard some creative ones. A British army officer thought he could arrange the use of their biggest helicopter that "should lift it." They would put slings under it that "would probably hold it" and they would just pick it up and set it in. Even if the boat wasn't damaged or destroyed in the process, my heart would have been. Another less risky suggestion was to load it on a low-boy trailer and truck it to the nearby Rio

Grande, but there were no ramps or cranes to launch it upon arrival.

We decided to stay with our theme of keeping it simple and also close to the ground. The boat would have to be backed out of the shed, then turned ninety degrees and moved 75 yards down a slope through the old horse pasture to the water's edge. I rented a backhoe from the Public Works department and had the lowest part of our bank cut down into a ramp that dropped five feet in its twenty-five foot length. We would build a stout cradle beneath the hull and move it slowly on pipe rollers. I had a lot of confidence in this part of the process, but the real challenge would be the launching itself. We would need to continue to move the boat another seventy-five yards from shore before it would float. I considered building the cradle in such a way it could be sheathed in plastic sheeting and be used as a shallow draft barge. Somehow I would sink it in an organized fashion once it was in deep water. It seemed anything but simple.

Carlos thought we could continue the same rolling process in the water, but the bottom was soft in places and I felt we would need a big source of power to get us through the muck. I checked into renting a log skidder, planning to employ its powerful winch. I found out it would be very expensive, and I wouldn't be allowed to operate it. I shuddered at the thought of a heavy-handed operator pulling everything apart. Carlos figured we could do it ourselves with the little cable-drum winch I had.

I was in the habit of being guided by my own judgment, but in working with Carlos and watching him build his house, I could see his engineering skills were greater than mine. He was not a formally-trained engineer, so was not bound by convention. The jungle had been his classroom, and he grew up moving logs and heavy dories using only ropes, rollers, wedges, and pry poles. Those experiences helped develop skills that came to him naturally. If he thought we could launch it by hand, then I was willing to give it a try. It was going to be a delicate and nerve-wracking operation no matter what, but by doing it ourselves we could work at our own pace.

During the last five years, the shop building and the boat shed had served as a cocoon, but now the butterfly was ready to emerge and the buildings had to be dismantled. The old shop was removed completely, the boat shed floor was taken up, and construction of the cradle was started. Under the hull, planks were laid on the ground to serve as tracks, and five twelve-foot pipes, each five inches in diameter, were spaced and laid crosswise on top. A stout framework, twelve by sixteen feet, was assembled on the pipes. Now the perilous task of lowering the boat began.

On each side, cables were run from the chain plates to the base of a tree and tensioned. The overhead and bilge supports were removed. A beam under the forward end of the keel, with high-lift jacks at each end, took the weight of the hull, and the keel supports were knocked out. The hull and our hearts were precariously suspended on two thin cables and two thin jacks. Carlos on his jack and I on mine lowered the hull one click; Christie on one cable puller and Tina on the other took up a half inch slack in the cables. Click by click and inch by inch the hull was lowered until she at last rested on the cradle. All of us were sweating but not from exertion. Bilge supports were fastened in place, and the cables were released—we were ready to roll.

The ground was smoothed where the old shop had been, and track beams were laid down. The drum winch was mounted on a stout frame that could be attached to either end of the cradle, and the cable was run out and back through a block attached to a tree. I wound the slack out of the cable, and then applied all my strength to the winch handle—the boat didn't move. We had only twenty yards to pull uphill before we could turn and start down toward the sea. If I couldn't move it on this slight incline, how could I expect to move it over the soft sea bottom? While I was considering my options, Carlos walked over, grabbed the taut cable and pulled sideways—the boat moved six inches! I never figured out what physical principle was at work; it didn't seem to be a lever, a screw or an inclined plane, nevertheless, we employed this technique during the entire process. By evening we had moved the boat into position under a big bullywood tree where we would set the masts in place.

Next morning I seriously wished for a prehensile tail as I perched on a branch forty feet above the boat. I hung a four-part block and tackle and gratefully returned to *terra firma*. With the tackle Carlos lifted the foremast, wrapped in stays, shrouds and halyards, and I guided the butt end through the partners and into its socket. It was that easy! We rolled the boat forward and repeated the procedure with the main/topmast unit. It was a thrill to finally see her all together, and we savored the sight before we started rigging her up.

My sojourn on the ground was brief as I was soon hauled aloft in the bosun chair to connect the masthead stays. Back on deck I rove the lanyards through the deadeyes and tensioned them. *Deadeyes and lanyards*—the phrase has a ring of piracy to it, and it should, for this system of tensioning mast shrouds is, like parceling and serving, centuries old. For us it suited the style of the schooner, but more importantly, it eliminated the need for expensive turnbuckles. The lanyard and the upper and lower deadeyes simply act as a block and tackle unit to tighten each shroud

The masts were over-raked by positioning their butts at the forward end of their slotted sockets. Then the forestay was tensioned until the fore and main masts were at their designed angles of five and seven degrees, respectively. The idea was to employ the spring and rake to avoid the need for backstays. The aft sides of both masts had straightened and they looked good.

We had received our first hard rain of the season the night before—three inches in a couple hours. It hadn't softened the ground, but the next one would; it was time to get to the water side. Carlos mowed a swath in the tall grass, and we started on the final sixty-yard trip to the ramp. Turning the cradle required jacking it up and setting the fore and aft rollers at opposing angles. Without trees to hook to, we set out the big Luke anchor and winched ourselves to it, repeating the procedure until we made the final turn at the head of the ramp. The easy part of the move was over.

Christie had been walking the ballast bars to the ramp in her bike basket, and after countless trips, she joined Tina in putting two coats of antifouling paint on the bottom. Carlos and I cleared away branches that overhung the ramp and did some underwater scouting for the best route to deep water. A soft muddy spot near shore couldn't be avoided; we would have to hope for the best. In late evening, we set up the gear for going down the steep ramp.

In the mountains across the bay, there had been rumbling during the night but no rain. The sun rose into a clear sky; we were being given one more dry day. The four of us were exhausted from days of backbreaking work, and it was a welcome site when our friend, Dale, showed up with Scott Forsyth to give us a hand. I didn't want to think of what would happen if this heavy tonnage got away from us on the steep ramp. Prudence and patience would be our guiding words. I dug in the big Luke astern and rove the cable while Carlos rigged a safety chain. Christie and Tina stood by on each side with wedges that *might* stop the cradle in an emergency.

The other three men edged the cradle forward with pry poles, while I eased the cable an inch at a time. She teetered for an instant on the brink, the weight came off the front roller and it shot down the ramp and into the water. The cradle settled on the incline with a jerk, and the cable parted. After a split second, the boat felt her freedom, and decided to chase the errant roller. But her liberty was brief as the safety chain caught and held her as it stretched bar taut; Christie and Tina quickly chocked the rollers. There were sighs and head shakes but little discussion; we all knew what had almost happened. I added more clamps to the cable connection and with Carlos manning the safety chain we eased her down the slope without any more trouble.

The big anchor, with a long line, was carried out in the dinghy and hand-set in six feet of water eighty yards out. Small-diameter logs were placed crosswise in the soft area near shore and the tracks laid over them; if we can only get across, I prayed. The logs sank along with my heart as the weight of the cradle came on them. The whole boat was over the water now—we were at the point of no return. "The logs have hit something firm," Carlos said, "it'll cross," and it did.

We had won the race, just by a nose perhaps, but her keel was wet and we had won! Let the rainy season come! A final turn of the cradle was made fifty feet from shore just as the sun went down.

24

~~~

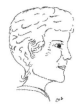

May 31, 1988

SPARK OF LIFE

In anticipation of this momentous christening day, Kirby and I had spent many evenings discussing names. It had been difficult to find an appropriate one that we could both agree on. That wasn't too surprising since this enterprise had from the beginning represented different things to each of us. Yet, as the project progressed, we both felt an evolving personality in this creation. We knew there was a special name that would suit her if we could just discover it.

I started out with the obvious—*Simplicity*. The *National Fishermen* had described this design as such. Yet we complicated it by adding top mast, bulwarks, quarter rails, davits and ratlines. This vessel was not as simple as Pete intended. Cross off number one.

Harmony, a nice description of the relationship we felt with this developing entity. "Too common," was Kirby's response.

I tried something that sounded traditional, *K. T. Rose*, with a nod toward the rosewood that had helped finance her building and would continue to maintain her. It would suit her old-fashioned look. Kirby shook his head, "Too egocentric."

"What about *Gypsy Rose?*" I always thought that Gypsy blood was the best explanation for my wanderlust.

"Wasn't she a lady of the night? People will think our boat is a brothel."

"How about *Dalbergia Rose?*" (Belizean rosewood— *Dalbergia Stevensonii)* I ventured. He shook his head.

"What about *Patience or Endurance?* Plenty of both have been required for this endeavor."

Nothing clicked. I kept trying.

Felicity? Yes, there was joy, and this name could have been embraced readily before VOA. But not anymore—she had much more purpose now.

"What about *Tomorrow's Noon,* like in the national anthem, 'for freedom comes tomorrow's noon?'" I had to look him in the eye to see if he was serious. He was. I shook my head.

Finally Kirby said, "I think we had better put a blackboard on the transom. We can switch names back and forth depending on our mood."

In the evening while re-reading Pete's book, *Spray,* a phrase jumped out at him. He turned to me, "This just might be it. Pete writes about learning the wind systems and how to use them. He tells how the old coastermen would wait for a favorable wind. They called it a *chance along.*"

I pondered. The name felt right. Being patient enough to wait a *chance along* embraced many of the words we had been considering: simplicity, harmony, tradition, mobility, endurance, awareness of the elements and the Belizean experience. Beyond that it implied the presence of a mystical force, something beyond our ability to control and it expresses this boat's character and our sailing philosophy to a T. Right away I picked up pen and paper to make a design for name boards.

We didn't share the schooner's name with visitors and we waited to attach the name signs as part of the launch ceremony. When the time came I watched as Kirby screwed the last fastening into place and stepped back. We looked at the overall effect. "Hum, nice!" we agreed and shared a hug. I hung a shell necklace on the figurehead, and Kirby ran up the Belizean flag while singing the national anthem. I gave a very short speech thanking in absentia the many people who had contributed to the process and asking that she and her crew would always have safe passages. I swung the bottle of Champagne against the stem fitting—it didn't break; Kirby tried it twice with the same result. We all laughed—ceremonies required skills we had never developed. Kirby popped the cork and I doused the figurehead, took a swig then handed the bottle back. Saluting the vessel, he took his swallow and handed the bottle to Christie and Carlos.

This was the fourth, and we hoped, final day of the long, drawn-out, launching procedure. *Chance Along* waited fifty feet out in the water, the wavelets gently lapping the cradle. It had dawned clear with a cool land breeze. Kirby set the smaller anchor and linked it to the big Luke with chain. If we became stuck, he hoped the two would be able to handle the pull without dragging. The line was tied to the deck windlass and the winch cable was hooked up directly to the chain. We continued the same procedure: every four feet we stopped to move the back roller, as it was released, to the front and every twelve feet we did the same with the track. It was exhausting work for an already-tired crew so Scott Forsythe was a welcome sight when he reappeared with fresh energy and a strong back. It was critical that we not get careless and let the cradle come off the rollers; jacking it up in the soft bottom might be impossible.

All went well until Archimedes started getting into the act. Our wooden track kept floating out of position and we had to weigh it down with sand bags. We encountered a few rocks and had to dig them out to smooth our road—still we continued.

The winch became submerged and to manipulate the rollers we had to duck under the muddy water and work by feel. Our own buoyancy was starting to become an issue but the schooner, though lighter, still sat firmly on the cradle. Just before the situation became untenable, the front of the cradle started lifting. We put down another set of tracks and let the rollers go out the back. She continued to lighten, and just before we reached the anchors she at last floated free. We untied the floating cradle and pushed it out from under her, and gracefully she swung to the light, sea breeze.

I lie here exhausted, unable to sleep. The slight movement, as *Chance Along* dips to the breeze, is soothing, and the quiet chuckles, as the wavelets caress her, is music I have long been waiting to hear. Kirby's gentle snores tell me he has given in to fatigue despite the excitement of our first night aboard our newly-launched vessel.

She leaked a gallon or two during the first hour, and now her planks are "taking up" nicely—there is very little water in the bilge. "Good job on the planking and caulking, Love," I whisper. From the cabin sole where we have spread our hastily-arranged bedding (we forgot the bunk boards) I can see the mainmast scribe an arc across a sky of twinkling stars. I send a telepathic message to the sleeping form snuggled against me, "We did it, Kirby; we did it! Here she is, floating." Tears of joy and relief give me much needed release. Gratitude wells up to consume me. I feel the presence of all those who helped along the way; I reach out to Christie and Carlos who so unstintingly gave us their time and energy and Scott for his continued encouragement. Dear, generous Jed and Sarah have been with us in spirit, as well as Pete, our guardian angel. It was disappointing to not share these moments with all those who had participated, but we had had to face our limitations.

"This is not going to be a smoking tallow kind of launch where dry to wet takes only a few seconds. A party would just add tension to an already loaded situation." All of Kirby's fears had surfaced in those words. I knew he was right. Then the clincher came, "The truth is, we have no money for a big celebration." Now, lying under the stars I realize that the true moment of celebration had occurred several weeks before the launch.

While poring over builder's codes, enacting marine traditions, reading sailor's myths, solving problems in three dimensions, there had been ever-present, an indefinable force; for me the whole process included a mystical aspect. It seemed as if this vessel was fastened together as much by enchantment as by screws, nails and bolts.

Despite having little skill with woodworking tools, when Kirby handed me the piece of wood to shape a figurehead, I felt confident—as if I had just been endowed with a special talent. I went through the process of sketching the shape and scaling the pattern to size. My few artistic skills were coalescing in this task. I penciled the pattern onto the face of the wood and cut the shape out on the band saw. With mallet and chisel I chipped away the rough edges and rounded them with a rasp. For the first time I experienced what came naturally to Kirby—a balance between eye, hand, and tool. Taking up the small disk sander, I shaped and smoothed the larger curves. With sandpaper and pad I did the final smoothing and finished with primer and several coats of white paint.

During the five years invested in this puzzle of timber, fastenings, goos, and glues there had been something fermenting within me. It was as if the gathering energy demanded expression through my heart and hands. I was astonished at what I had created; the form was that of a live creature and the curves were sensuous to the touch.

I continued to work in a fever of mind and spirit. Taking the smallest paint brush, I painted her eyes blue. With a tiny touch of white enamel on the pupils, a sparkle appeared and I felt a zap of electricity—a spark of life. Suddenly these eyes were magical, ready to guide us among the many reefs and cays of the blue, sometimes turquoise waters of Belize.

Holding our breaths we raised the dolphin into place. The fastenings drew her tightly into the corner between stem post and bow sprit. Suddenly we felt a shift in the energy field and the space around us was filled with her presence; this vessel we had created out of wood felt as if it had come alive. Kirby whispered, "I feel like Gippetto must have when Pinocchio became a real boy."

Pouring Miss Lois's cashew wine, raising rosewood goblets in salute, we toasted this birthing "To Chancy. May your spirit and sonar guide us safely wherever we journey."

With that awe-inspiring memory and the realization that tomorrow would be the beginning of a whole new way-of-life, I finally surrendered to a deep and satisfying sleep.

SALTWATER SAILS AND SUNSETS

"...there is a certain appeal to the risk-taking and like any form of gambling, sailing has an addictive element." KGS

25
~~~

January -- August 1989

EXPANDED HORIZONS

The portents were auspicious—a new moon and beautiful weather. I was bubbling with excitement—and trepidation. The time had finally come to move aboard; were we ready?

This moment had been delayed a few weeks; immediately after the launch, we had travelled to Montana to attend Kirby's parents' golden anniversary. The time away gave us a much-needed break from the intensity of those pre-launch months and a fresh perspective. In comparison to 50 years of marriage, building a boat was a small accomplishment, but the five year project had tested and strengthened our own relationship, a bonus we hadn't expected. Despite, or maybe because of, the struggle to finish this long, drawn-out venture, we had become more than ever committed to each other and to the dream we shared.

Back at Orange Point we were preparing for the first sail. "Come on, Babe," Kirby beckoned. He had been rowing out the last of the ballast. Dipping one oar he made a tidy turn about and I got in.

"There's a breeze—let's go sailing!"

"But we haven't rigged the sails yet."

"We have the jib and mainstays'l and I can't wait to see how she moves."

We stowed the lead bars under the cabin sole between the floor timbers; *Chance Along* had settled two inches lower than expected. Our use of heavy tropical timbers in the hull construction was the likely explanation, but her fore and aft trim was perfect, and she looked right. Compared to *Sunalee,* when I stepped aboard, she felt like a ship.

We attached the jib and lower mainstays'l to their halyards and sheet lines and hoisted them. It was late morning, the land breeze had retired after an eight hour shift, and the sea breeze was reluctantly taking over. To prepare for the possibility of poor performance, we told ourselves not to expect much; the two sails had very little area, and the breeze was light. Anxiously we hauled the anchor, backed the jib, and turned her broadside to the wind. She hesitated, somewhat theatrically I thought, and then gradually picked up momentum, sliding easily through the water and leaving almost no wake.

"She's sailing!" I shouted.

"Like a lady," Kirby said as he took me in his arms.

It was such a wonderful feeling! It wasn't that I ever doubted she would be moved by the wind, but what a disappointment it would have been if we had spent five years building a sluggard. No words were needed to describe our elation. Our first date with *Chance Along* was a thrill, the beginning of a love affair.

I had whetted my appetite for sailing by absorbing books on how to live aboard sailing vessels—specifically ocean cruisers. Therefore my tendency was to prepare for an extended voyage. Taking too little seemed more of a problem than taking too much, but I still had to find a way to store the stores. Even though *Chance Along* was cavernous compared to *Sunalee,* she had no cupboards or closets, and my pig tail buckets provided minimal storage. Still, many of the dry goods and cans fit in under the bunks. The fresh produce was hung in small hammocks and

I tucked the pressure cooker and other pots and pans behind a vertical board. My little stove was the center of the galley; the butane bottle was just outside the companionway where it could easily be turned off after each use. The small amount of clothing we needed would be kept in baskets at the foot of the bunks. The bunks had two-inch sponge mattresses, spartan but adequate. All in all, the cabin filled our basic needs without feeling crowded.

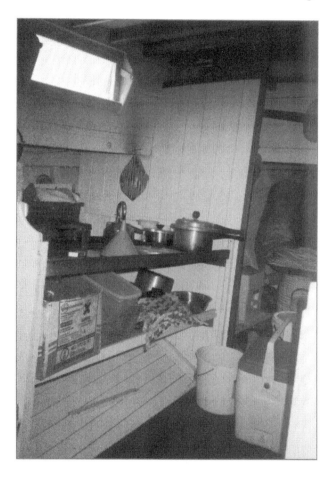

Each box, bag and can we brought aboard had to be loaded, stored, used, and then unloaded since we wouldn't consider throwing trash in the sea. We soon became conscious of how much fresh water we used for bathing and washing clothes (about four gallons per day) and every morsel of food and sip of liquid we put into our mouths. For people who were trying to have a small "footprint," we sure seemed to consume a lot.

In the end, I had to re-evaluate my expectations for provisioning. After all, we would seldom be out of sight of land or more than a day's sail away from supplies. Luckily, I had Maurice Griffith's delightful books on coastal cruising to help me keep perspective.

But having adequate boat gear was one area we weren't willing to compromise, and we had to make room for each item. Spare anchors (a local fisherman and a Danforth) and lines were stowed in the forepeak along with the extra life vests. The lead line hung near the companionway ladder. Kirby made a special rosewood bowl with a domed lid for the compass and attached it to the aft bulkhead where the helmsman could easily read it. The handheld compass and binoculars were stowed in holders just inside the aft cabin within easy reach of the cockpit. Perhaps we carried more ground tackle than necessary, but we were convinced that we shouldn't be out on the water if we couldn't take care of ourselves. Our gear was simple but strong, appropriate, and easily cared for.

It was gratifying to see that the details we had spent so much effort on were actually functional. The bitts were large and well-placed for working the anchor lines. The davits were a sensible way to deal with the dinghy in our waters behind the barrier reef. The dead eyes were well-suited for her short, stout masts and gave her a salty look, in harmony with the rest of the vessel. The trim tab was a blessing; it helped keep the course and eased the tiller when under power.

With the basics for living in place, it was time to meet our obligations. By borrowing the money to complete *Chance Along*, we had speeded up our launching timetable considerably. We had danced to the music, but now it was time to pay the piper. We turned the bow toward Jed and Sarah's place. Thoughts of sailing had to be put on hold.

It was a remote area, one we had visited a few times aboard *Sunalee* with her much shallower draft. Tensely, we left the main channel and headed west. From the marine charts, we knew it was studded with shoals lurking just below the surface. With Jed's instructions in mind, we eased our way along. The water was murky, and I was on the side deck casting the lead line to determine depth while Kirby steered. Low-lying clouds danced shadows across the water; only by watching for a few moments could we tell which dark areas were shoals—they didn't move. A thunderhead was puffing up over the western mountains, and squally weather could be expected as it expanded toward the sea. We hoped to be securely anchored in case it came our way. Should we hurry and risk grounding or go slowly and chance being caught out by darkness—just one of the many judgments we would have to continually make as sailors.

By the time we were within five or six hundred yards of the dock, *Chance Along's* keel, at five feet, had only a foot of water under it. Kirby pitched the anchor. It dug in easily and held well when backed in with the motor. The shoals that had presented a hazard during our approach now served to give us moderate protection from the afternoon chop. The thunderhead didn't seem to be a threat yet, so we donned appropriate clothing to discourage bugs and headed for shore.

It was awkward for us and for Jed and Sarah to make the necessary change of roles, from friends to employee and employer. They obviously wanted this experience to begin in the friendliest possible way, and after business they invited us to dinner. I tried to put aside my anxiety about the weather. Part way through the meal the thunder started rumbling, and soon the wind and rain were driving into the clearing. There was nothing to do but wait it out. Dessert was eaten and still the storm lingered, then darkness came. As soon as the wind eased up, we started out. These were the worst conditions for little *Oardeal*. We had borrowed Carlos' small, outboard engine for the duration of this job, but it was no match for the waves, and we had to tack back and forth to make any headway. We soon lost visibility which gave us poor odds of locating *Chance Along*. We turned back.

We weren't sure we could find the pier again, but we could at least shelter in the mangroves until the weather slackened a bit. Kirby's instincts turned out to be good, and soon we came alongside where our friends loomed out of the rain with helping hands. We were back aboard as soon as the weather cleared.

For Kirby the job was an endurance test. He hadn't worked for a real boss in eighteen years, and he chafed in the role of employee. But he kept reminding himself that we would not be afloat if our friends hadn't helped us with the loan. He enjoyed the carpentry work and was learning new skills using a chainsaw mill. Still, it was a welcome sound when the yellow tails (*Oropendolas*) started their evening gargling from the tree tops; it was a sign that the day would soon be finished, and he could get in the dinghy, shuck off boots and long clothes and return to our little home. He would mark off another day on the calendar, knowing that in a few months our obligation would be fulfilled, and we could go on with our dream.

In contrast I found my new life aboard very fulfilling. Frequently, *Chance Along* and I were visited by dolphins, and occasionally I caught sight of a manatee. The ibis, egrets, frigatebirds and pelicans each had daily cycles that became my way of keeping time. When the maintenance and household chores were done, I read from our collection of marine books. I studied the sail handling and maneuvering techniques we would need to develop, and I accumulated a fair knowledge of sea folklore. With my hand-cranked Singer, I sewed up sail, mattress, and cushion covers. Curtains and a matching wind scoop were the final touches that gave *Chance Along* the feeling of home.

Having a regular work schedule brought back our appreciation for weekends. There was so much to explore! I found the setting uniquely beautiful with lovely vistas in each compass quadrant. Verdant hills were close by with the blue Maya mountains in the background. A half mile away a small river cut through the mangrove-forested shoreline, and cays were scattered from south to northeast. The rediscovery of the night sky and the 360 degree horizon seemed to expand my spirit.

Chance Along has an easy motion, and though the sea was usually choppy by late afternoon, I soon became accustomed to the movement. It was harder for Kirby. Near midnight *Chance Along* swung to the land breeze, and the residual waves caused her to roll a little. Kirby says he woke up to the clink, clink of glass against glass, not loud but irritating to a light sleeper. He got up to investigate but just then it stopped. This phenomenon repeated itself several times. He knew it wasn't rational, but it seemed either the flashlight or his quick movement was frightening the source of the noise. Finally, by moving slowly and working in the dark, he found the culprits in the bottom of one of the pigtail buckets; two bottles were making music. Thus the first of our superstitions (every boat needs them) was born. Never store the Lea and Perrins next to the Maiden soy sauce, especially on a full moon.

Over the years we had worked out our roles on shore and in general they transferred naturally to boat life: I managed the provisioning and "household" affairs and Kirby had charge of the machinery and maintenance. But living together full time in such a small space took some adjustment and some organization. When he listened to the news or the talk shows on the radio and I wanted to write in the log book I had to move to the cockpit. If I was cooking he had to move to another space to write in his journal. We discovered whose bunk was most advantageous for love sessions and what areas served best as work spaces on deck. We each found our favorite nooks for reflection and solitude.

Sailing presented other challenges to our relationship. There are a multitude of judgments to make: how to get the most favorable wind, when to tack and when to reef, what course to take through shoal waters, and when and where to anchor. With time we learned to recognize our strengths and weaknesses. I am most effective up in the ratlines conning the boat through the reefs. Kirby is skilled at choosing the best anchoring spot in relation to other physical hazards: boats, reefs and cays. He can lose his concentration when in a conversation with guests, and if we are going through a tight passage it is best that I steer. He navigates using geographical features, whereas I make course judgments based on feel. In dawn's first light I imagine every dark cloud to represent a rain storm, and on the other end of the spectrum, Kirby is confident it will soon dissipate.

Compromise is often necessary, but in crisis situations there may be no time for discussion. When running down on a reef, any decision is better than none, and under those conditions Kirby takes command; I do my best to follow his orders. Like the talents required in other aspects of our life, our sailing skills are complementary—even synergistic.

Finally, the last day of work arrived. Kirby was up early to check the fishing line he had set out the night before. It was Floyd he was after. Floyd was a large Goliath grouper that had taken up residence under the hull a month before. Even when we took *Chance Along* away for a few days, Floyd soon appeared after our return. He was an arrogant fellow and seemed to enjoy slapping his large tail against the hull in a proprietary way. He could make the hull vibrate like a drum and for variety he occasionally thonked the propeller for its cymbal-like effect. The first time scared us out of our wits. Then we heard his song— whoop, who-o-op, who-o-o-op. Since these musical interludes could wake us from a sound sleep it was hard to fully appreciate the honor of his serenade.

Kirby would often put a line overboard in the evening to catch a catfish. In the morning he would sometimes have on the hook both the catfish and Floyd, the one inside the other. He would persuade Floyd to disgorge the catfish encouraging him to do his own fishing. Kirby would then take the partly digested fish into shore for bait for the work crew's fishing lines. Floyd never seemed to tire of this game; then again, Kirby didn't either.

But the time had come to end it and Kirby had put out a big hook on a heavy line. We knew that once we moved

Chance Along permanently, Floyd would go back to the cool shade of the dock and then would be prey to the many hooks just waiting for his beefy bulk. We decided we would fill our own cooking pot, and I got out the canner. As Kirby administered the coup de grâce he remarked, "The tables have turned on you, Floyd, and now it is your turn on the table."

We glanced back as we sailed out of the anchorage that had been our protection for several months; it had been a productive time. We had fulfilled our obligations and had made *Chance Along* into our home. We could expect numerous and unknown hazards between us and the horizon but adventure and discoveries too.

26

~~~

Fall 1989

BEAR ESSENTIALS

For almost three weeks I had been flat on my back in the bunk. I blamed the injury on my encounter with the Bear. Of course, I knew the issue was far more complex. We returned from our last visit to the States with a Portuguese Water Dog. Tina's research had convinced us that the breed was perfect for boat life. Since much of our sailing would be in remote areas, it would be nice to have an alert guard aboard. In addition, we always had dogs ashore and we would miss their companionship.

We had contacted the breed's Montana association; locally, no puppies were available but a four-year-old was. "Bear" had been rescued, from what we never found out, but we were assured that his present psychological problems would disappear once he was in a stable, loving environment. My dad's comment as a farmer was terse, "Cheap animals are usually trouble." I know he was basing this on the $50 jersey cow he bought from the neighbor— the one that routinely ran to the far end of the pasture just before milking time, and occasionally kicked us across the barn.

Our flight home was delayed, and to avoid the cost of a hotel, we spent two days camped in the New Orleans airport. Meeting Bear's needs under those conditions was a challenge, to say the least. I at last found a little patch of grass between two cement columns that met with Bear's approval. When we finally boarded, weather diverted our flight through San Salvador where I watched our luggage being transferred to the Belize flight. The cargo doors were closed, we received our boarding call, and still Bear's carrier remained on the cart. I dashed out the emergency exit and down onto the tarmac. After a frantic multilingual exchange with field personnel and then with security guards, I managed to avoid imprisonment and to get Bear loaded on the Belize flight. We knew he was aboard because we could hear him barking from somewhere in the bowels of the plane. So far our life with him had not started auspiciously.

Bear moved on board with us, and our bonding was immediate. He was the most affectionate dog we had ever had, and we fell in love with his spirit. Though the boat environment was completely foreign to him, he tried his best to adapt. He was alert and took his job as a guard seriously. He barked when any boat was in the vicinity, but he was particularly ferocious with creatures in the water. When I went spear fishing or was coming up from having scrubbed the propeller, he went wild at the sight of my snorkel. Whether he was preparing to attack or save me, I wasn't sure.

We were glad for his willingness to become part of the family, but he refused to be excluded at any time and our love life suffered. A furry head poking through the companionway with occasional yips of protest lends little to an atmosphere of intimacy. He attached himself to us so closely he suffered when we left him aboard alone, a serious flaw in our plans for his employment. He was a great swimmer and would plunge overboard whenever we entered the dinghy; occasionally he would beat us to shore. I wondered if a Chihuahua wouldn't have been a better choice. Tying him was the only solution we could think of, and even then, he barked continuously, alerting every would-be thief for miles.

My injury occurred on an already bad day. We were anchored in Yankee Doodle Bight, so named because from there we could once again hear the Voice of America program being broadcast. We would row ashore after breakfast, and walk the short distance across the point to Carlos's shop where I continued to do my lathe work. That day I had hiked into town to call the Fort George Hotel. Their check for my last shipment was long overdue, and our financial status was even bleaker than normal. The check had not been sent, they explained, because the order had not arrived. A call to the airline I had sent it on, produced the information that they accepted no responsibility. I was late returning, so Tina had gone ahead with the dinghy. I waded through the swamp with a flashlight, and she picked me up on the foreshore.

Though he had lived aboard for more than a year, Bear remained confused as to what proper, onboard etiquette was in regard to bodily functions. His use of the mat, which had been provided for that purpose, was sporadic; still we continued in our attempts to boat train him. I had just lain back with my novel when I heard the distinctive sound of a stream of liquid being released on the cabin top above my head. I flew out of the companionway in an effort to catch him in the act, and as I turned I was immobilized by a muscle spasm in my lower back that just wouldn't let up. Tina got me into my bunk where I remained in intense pain for the remainder of the night.

The next day the pain could be managed with aspirin, and I knew that I would eventually heal, but in the meantime any movement was torture. On the positive side was the rediscovery that I do my clearest thinking when I am in a weakened state. If I found truth only when my guard was down, was it only truth that my guard was protecting me from? The magnitude of the question was overwhelming, and I turned to a less philosophical topic.

Something was seriously wrong—something that I was not admitting to. Sure the loss of the order was a financial blow, but I had no doubt we would recover. After all, living hand-to-mouth had been a way of life since we had arrived in Belize. So the uptightness that had precipitated the injury had a deeper source. The debt was paid off and we were living on board, but there was little joy in it. Tina wasn't complaining even though she was at the moment carrying my load as well as hers. Still she wasn't happy. I wondered if the whole thing had been a mistake. The backyards and the backwater marinas of the world are full of boats, each representing the dissolution of someone's dream—boats whose owners have discovered in a painful way that one can get great pleasure out of building or buying a boat and still not enjoy sailing it. Could that be true of me, too?

I flashed back a few months to the schooner's trial run with all her working sails. Tina had backed the jib, and as the fore and mains'l filled, *Chance Along* started moving forward. Then gracefully she lowered her rail and went to work. Through the tiller I could feel her power and the thrill of it was beyond description. Except for my need for Tina, it is as close to an addiction as I've ever had. No, I had no doubt about the pleasures I got from sailing.

In fairness I had to admit we had ample reasons for being discouraged. Our financial circumstances had not changed for the better, and considering the added cost of maintaining a sailboat, they had been made worse. Now we lived aboard in conditions which were often uncomfortable. Our house had been allowed to biodegrade during the building process and was taken down shortly after we moved aboard, so now we were dependent on the generosity of our children to share their homes and work areas. These factors combined could certainly explain the stress-related health problems I was experiencing.

There were parallels here with the country of Belize. She had been given her freedom from Great Britain eight years earlier, but it was not obvious what had been gained. Perhaps, like us, all her energy was used up in the effort. The colonial laws and institutions that promoted resource exploitation weren't significantly changed nor had the living conditions for the average citizen improved. Belize was now responsible for paying her own bills, and devaluation of the currency was an ongoing worry. But Belize had achieved the right to make her own choices, and there were merits in just having that freedom.

Choices—that is what the boat gave us. On her we could reside in an unlimited number of locations. Our potential ways of making a living had increased, and she gave us the means to travel and explore the natural world of water. But it had become clear that we wanted more than the freedom of choice—we wanted to experience the benefits derived from exercising that freedom. To achieve the sense of well-being we were seeking, we would need to exert the same level of energy we had used in building the boat—it wasn't going to be reached just because we felt entitled or even if we believed we had earned it. So far, we had taken the path of least resistance—we had returned to Orange Point and were continuing to do what we had always done while awaiting the arrival of some state of carefree bliss.

Also affecting our attitudes was the neglect of that element of creativity that had been so much a part of the boatbuilding. We could claim to be experiencing something similar to "writer's block," but more honestly, we had just been letting old habits take over. Employing our creativity was the most effective way to improve our situation, but more importantly, it was an essential ingredient for maintaining a positive outlook.

I reminded myself that the dream was to explore this wet world that had been our front yard for so many years—to get to know it like we had gotten to know the forest, to see it, but more importantly, to feel its vibrations. The first step of the dream had been achieved. Now we were facing a new challenge; we had built and launched this vehicle of freedom—could we live up to her potential? It was going to require all the energy and creative juices we could squeeze out.

Gradually my back healed and I started doing craft work again, but now with a more positive attitude. I started gathering the tools that would allow me to work on board. I built a little lathe that could be used in the cockpit, but for our longer range plans, I modified my shop lathe to fit in the aft cabin and built a small band saw device that could be attached for cutting the turning blanks. Our little portable generator would power it all, and I worked on a new type of muffler system to quiet it down.

The bight provided fair protection from the prevailing sea breeze, but the swells swept around the point and made for a very rolly anchorage. We could reduce the roll by using a stern anchor to hold us bow-on to the swell, but that left us broadside and vulnerable to the night storms. A good night's rest had become a rare event. The situation was untenable and we decided we would have to find another base.

Twenty miles up the coast was New Haven Bay. It had no road access, was far from any stores, and was noted for its lightning storms. But it is a natural harbor about a half mile across and is well protected from all but south winds. Charlie had recognized its potential when he arrived with his big sloop *Endymion*. We had used his marine railway to haul out *Sunalee* and more recently *Chance Along*. Its remoteness and the fact the shore was plagued with sand flies had discouraged development and Charlie and his family were the only fulltime residents. It could make a good base for *Chance Along*, and with all the negative factors, it might be affordable.

After some negotiations, Mr. Alan, who owned a small parcel on the bay, agreed to sell us two acres and accept payments. It was up to us to do all the paperwork. I did a title search in Belize City and then found someone to draw up the transfer papers. In Belmopan I made the rounds of government offices to get permission for the sale, and in Punta Gorda I located a man who was willing to do the survey. It would take time to establish a new base, but it felt good to be back on course again, working near our maximum potential, revising and then proceeding toward our dream, one step at a time.

Though he was indirectly responsible for my injury, it was impossible to look into the depths of Bear's eyes and hold a grudge. During my convalescence, he had been my stalwart companion, as he had been for Tina during the time I was working off our debt. His bathroom habits improved somewhat, and he no longer decorated the deck with his "land mines." Early one morning, I was forward in the head, and at my request, Tina gave Bear a roll of toilet paper which he proudly delivered to me. It wasn't brandy and he wasn't a St. Bernard but it was welcome just the same. Except for offering his companionship, it was the first worthwhile thing he had done since he joined the crew—there was still hope. Perhaps we could even incorporate him into the KirbyKraft business: I would turn the bowl, Tina would finish it, and Bear would lick the sticker to go on the bottom.

27

~~~

NEW HAVEN—NEW LIFE

As we approached New Haven, I recognized several of the boats at anchor. We were always a bit self-conscious when we knew others were watching our seamanship, and a sailboat is a great device for making a public fool out of one's self. So we were tacking carefully.

In the broad entrance of the bay, we were met by a pair of dolphins who zoomed over to investigate our bow wave. Bear got excited with snorkelers, but with dolphins he went berserk. When they ignored his frantic barking from the foredeck, he decided he would have to get closer by walking out the narrow and pitching bowsprit. He managed about two steps before he lost his balance. His strategy was effective—the dolphins *did* disappear when a barking, furry mass fell almost on their heads. We performed a very lubberly, dog-overboard maneuver which resulted in the boat making a complete circle with her sails flogging, a soggy dog racing around the deck in an attempt to get dry, and the crew getting drenched. We got underway again, made a few more smooth tacks which we hoped would polish our tarnished image and dropped anchor in front of our new place.

It was the time of year when cruising boats came to enjoy Belize's barrier reef or to make their way back north after spending a few months on the Rio Dulce. (That

Guatemalan river is only a day's sail away and has become the favorite "hurricane hole" for this part of the Caribbean.) From one of the nearby visitors, we heard an outboard engine come to life, and soon a middle-aged man approached in his inflatable dinghy. "Beautiful boat," he said. "How old is she?"

"We launched her two years ago at Orange Point," I answered.

"Oh." He sounded a bit crestfallen.

Chance Along's traditional good looks brought her many compliments, but people were always disappointed to find out she wasn't old.

This was his first time in the bay, and he had a lot of questions. We did too, having never talked to anyone who sailed with a Chinese junk rig. The conversation continued while we cleared the deck. There were dwarf coconut sprouts, small containers with fruit tree seedlings and a big bag of chicken manure. On the other side were a few boards, concrete blocks and a sheet of metal roofing. It would be considered a very unusual cargo on a cruising boat, the norm being barbeque grills, fuel jugs and kayaks. It was the last item that caused our new acquaintance to leave. It was just too much sacrilege for his romantic heart to see us use the schooner's halyard to lower an old lawn mower into the dinghy.

The cruising people we met had to be self-sufficient types to ever make it this far. We admired this characteristic and also their community spirit. They were generous with sailing tips and were always willing to help anyone in trouble. We enjoyed them most on a one-on-one basis. We shared sailing experiences, discussed the characteristics of our boats, weather patterns and anchorages; sometimes our conversations covered more personal topics such as finances and family. But when we visited with cruisers in a crowd, we were often uncomfortable. The group setting and a few drinks seemed to bring out our differences. We could not condone, much less applaud, those who filled their freezers with out-of-season lobster or fish; we refused to participate in the verbal bashing of misunderstood, Belizean behavior and we had little knowledge or interest in the latest electronic gadgetry.

On the contrary, we took pride in the simplicity of our gear and equipment. Keeping it simple was the only way we could afford to maintain the boat—it was also a concept we believed in. With no docks to tie to, we always rode to an anchor, and our ground tackle was simple, strong, and in good condition. The sturdy, hand-cranked windlass was slow but powerful, and with few moving parts it was reliable and easy to maintain. Our "depth sounder" required no batteries, wires or electricity—it was a lead weight on a line like old-time sailors used; the only moving part was one of our arms to cast it alongside *Chance Along*. With a knot for the first fathom (six feet), two knots for the second and so forth, the water depth was easily determined. It would also quickly indicate whether or not the anchor was holding. Sophisticated navigational equipment was not required since we were almost always within sight of land, but we continually honed our piloting skills using the hand-bearing compass and a set of good charts.

Most cruising boats are built of fiberglass or steel, and it is commonly believed they are cheaper to maintain than a wooden boat. With our previous boats we had already experienced the need for continuous maintenance to keep the fresh water out above the waterline and the toredo worms out below. But it was work we could do ourselves, and I was glad not to be repairing fiberglass and maintaining auto pilots, electric winches, navigational equipment, refrigeration units and the generators required to keep it all running. Our boat is biodegradable like everything else in Nature (including ourselves) and that somehow seems right.

The fundamental difference between us and the transient cruisers was that we weren't going anywhere. Belize had been our home for nearly twenty years, and we felt protective of her resources and her people.

New Haven had probably been an excellent base for Mr. Alan's grandfather and great-uncle who had come from the Bay Islands of Honduras in the late 1800's with their two large schooners. Each brother bought 100 acres on the bay from the British Crown. The families thrived by producing children, pigs, and copra and by freighting products from the area, mainly sugar and timber. The two acres we bought had many cashew, mango, and coconut trees and an 8 by 12-foot shack.

The fact the old building was still standing was apparently due to the reinforcing effect of the termite runners on the posts—nature's Kevlar. I did a lot of diagonal bracing and reorganized the holes in the metal roofing so there was a small dry area to set my lathe under. *Chance Along* was anchored 75 yards offshore, and I commuted with *Oardeal*. We received the full benefit of the sea breeze, and when it was blowing, insects were not a problem.

CHANCE ALONG

Charlie lived a half mile up the shore. His wife had decamped with their five children, the isolation and difficult living conditions finally getting the best of her. He had a sidekick in our friend Ron and a new lady, Patty, who added a womanly touch to what had become a bachelor pad. Ron played a big role in keeping the place on an even keel and the boat yard operational. As he had at Orange Point, he was willing to give us a hand when we needed it, and his droll sense of humor was always welcome. I once overheard him introduce the New Haven bunch to a recently-arrived sailor: "Over there is Hard Luck Charlie and PMS Patty. I'm Long Gone Ron."

Charlie's storytelling abilities were legendary throughout the boating community, and this reputation was as influential as the harbor itself in attracting cruising boats. People came just so they could tell their friends they had met him. His often outrageous and unpredictable behavior was an effective deterrent to would-be troublemakers, which of course was a benefit to us. But he was generous and a good host and he could always get volunteers to help when there was a boat to haul up. He earned the name "Hard Luck" not from misfortune but from his "poor me" stories.

He had a large circle of sailing friends who were periodic visitors to the bay. Quite a number were based on the Rio Dulce so were new acquaintances for us. But we had already met most of the Belizean boaters. Tina Hess came through on her trips from Placencia to the Rio and sometimes hauled her sloop, *Baby Cake*. Diana was an occasional visitor aboard her sloop, *Enchilada,* or sometimes as crew on someone else's boat. Marcia came with the renowned little sloop, *Miss Lady,* and Mike and Bonny on their trimaran, *Adios.* Chris was in the bay frequently while doing charters with his old wooden sharpie, *Juanita.* Nick brought his schooner, *Miss Lou,* every year or so to be hauled out and painted. Arturo and Linda chartered in the area with their big ketch, *Tangaroa.*

John and Bonny worked in the area and often anchored their ketch, *Phalcor*, in the bay. Norm had his sloop, *Placencia*, on a mooring in Ron's care as did Sid with *Suppoze II*. Both Sid and Norm spent time at New Haven seasonally.

This was Charlie's turf—he and his family had been the only residents in the bay for many years, and though we were landowners, we were also newcomers and we tried to keep that in mind. We had known Charlie and his family since they first arrived, and now a good neighborly relationship developed. We usually gathered together for birthdays and holiday celebrations and occasionally accepted a ride to town in his skiff. We had ample opportunity to socialize aboard friends' vessels, and we sold our wares to visitors when the opportunity arose. Every ten days or two weeks, we would haul anchor and sail to Placencia or Punta Gorda for provisions and visits to friends and family.

When the lawn mower and building supplies were finally ashore, I rowed to the upper end of the bay to see Sid. He had arrived the previous week for a ten day stay and had sent me a note regarding a building project. We needed to broaden our financial base and I wasn't going to miss the chance to do so.

Sid owned a few acres and had built a small thatched structure on pilings a few dozen yards off shore. In this way he avoided the sand flies and got enough water depth to tie his sloop alongside. He wasn't interested in sailing, but he was proud of his boat and had rigged her with high-quality gear. The interior was functional but plain, and he wanted me to remodel it—cut out part of the bulkheads, add some turned spindles and install a rosewood dinette. The income would augment our craft earnings, and much of the work could be done at New Haven. "How much do you want to pay?" I asked.

"Whatever you charge me," he answered, "but if it is too high I just won't hire you again." Spoken like a businessman, I thought, but not a bad philosophy.

In spite of his abrupt manner, he had a great sense of humor. He claimed he was the *fastest pun* in his part of Texas. In the cabin was a plaque that read:

Suppoze II
Four C's Yachts
Caribbean Custom Coastal Cruisers
Sonova Beach, Belize

On their previous visit, Sid and his wife Karlyn were trying to think of a good name for their property. They both liked to sunbathe, and in a moment of inspiration I suggested *Toucan Strip*. He liked the name and even had a little sign made up, but always felt bad that he hadn't thought of it himself.

We completed the plan for the remodeled cabin and shook hands on the deal. I planned to have the work finished before his next visit. He had been very successful at buying and selling property in Austin and had a good grasp of human nature. "If you really want a life on the water," he advised, "you will get rid of your property at Orange Point." He was probably right, but it was a bridge that we weren't ready to burn—at least not yet.

28
~~~

January 1990

KITH AND KIN

Because Kirby had been a hunter while growing up, fishing with a spear gun came more naturally to him than trolling or hand lining, but it was not the kind of fishing best suited to New Haven's hazy waters. Ron was an excellent fisherman, and he was generous in passing on his knowledge. Gradually, Kirby started picking up the rhythm of the place and fish became an important element in our diet both nutritionally and financially.

At first light he would load the dinghy with cast net, a trolling line and his box of hooks, sinkers and hand lines. He would rig up and sail into the northeast corner of the bay where the bait fish gathered. Finding bait was as much an art as fishing itself and it was all part of the process. If it went quickly he might come back to *Chance Along* for breakfast before heading out to his favorite "drop." He usually filled me in on the smallest detail of the morning's bait gathering—how the pelicans led him to the right spot, the speed of the mullet that eluded him, and the lucky cast that filled his net with sprat.

If the wind was blowing even a bit, he would sail to whichever spot he thought would be best, pulling the trolling lure along behind. When without wind, he would wrap the line around the handle of the oar, and as he pulled, the lure would jerk, enticing a nice sized fish to take a chance. Once, through the field glasses, I saw him hook a large barracuda while under full sail. Later he described the event as pure chaos—the line wrapping around the rudder as the big fish ran, the boom swinging over and knocking him in the head, the boat ramming into the mangroves, and finally hauling the beast aboard while trying to keep his bare feet from getting sliced by the slashing teeth.

On his return, I would meet him at the rail as he sailed alongside, take his painter (bow line), and playing my role in an ages-old drama would ask, "Well, did you have any luck?" Once in a great while he would depressingly reply that he had been skunked. But usually his face would light up with the joy of achievement; he would slowly take the life cushion off the top of his bucket, as if to keep me in anticipation just a moment longer, and then hold up the biggest of the day's catch for my admiration. Just as important as catching the fish, was the replay as he told me each little detail of the experience. I always listened as if it were the first time. That's just what you do when you love your man.

Up before dawn, spending the morning out in the heat and sun, patiently baiting his hooks again and again as if time did not matter; I had to stretch my imagination as to why this activity gave him such delight. For some, fishing is the essence of escape, but for Kirby it seemed to be the challenge of it all. He learned where the banks of rocks were and could tell when he was over them by listening for the crackle in the handle of his oar. He tried to tune in to all the nuances of Nature—tides, position of the sun and moon, the kind of bait, the water temperature, salinity and clarity, and learned to accept the fact that sometimes they just wouldn't bite.

People have fished with simple gear since the beginning of time and it has required the same knowledge of the environment that Kirby was trying to acquire. Only in rather recent times has fishing employed huge nets pulled by powerful boats where fish are caught in huge quantities whether they are hungry or not and the fisherman's knowledge of machines is more important than his understanding of Nature. "Progress" seems to have become a measure of humankind's success in circumventing Nature's rules. But in fishing, and perhaps in most other cases, bypassing the natural requirement for balance leads only to *temporary* success—the biggest of nets will catch nothing once all the fish are gone.

We would occasionally take a day off from shop work, hoist *Chance Along*'s sails and head out into the deeper waters around the Snake Cays, the troll lines streaming out behind. It was enough just to be sailing but the chance of hooking a big one made it an adventure. More than once a good-sized fish took the lure just as we were approaching Punta Ycacos on our return.

Sails out wing and wing, we would be flying downwind into the narrow inner channel—approaching the time when all hands would be needed to make a controlled jibe. When the breeze was fresh our actions had to be coordinated to prevent damage to the gear and or even loss of steering control. Kirby would haul the mains'l in tight to limit the swing of the boom and I would gradually change course until the wind caught the sail on the opposite side. I would be fighting for control of the helm while Kirby was letting the sail out—it was during that moment that the fish liked to hit the lure. Then chaos reigned until we hauled the fish aboard, lines coiled, and our sails reset to make our anchorage in the bay.

New Haven offered other treats in addition to fish. There were the fruits planted by Mr. Alan's family: coconuts, mango, cashew and pineapples. Wild fruits came at varying times of the year: hog plums, sea grapes, coco plum, and there was a blackberry tree near the boatyard well. All of these made delicious jams and jellies even though some puckered the mouth when eaten fresh. One of the best ways to preserve the fruit was to make wine. The sea grape received the most raves. When it came out right there was a slight hint of sea salt that made it unique. At a gathering, Charlie would make *chicha*—a lightly fermented grain brew—and Ron always seemed to be able to produce a grouper and knew how to cook it to perfection. But it wasn't the bounty or socializing that made me recognize I had found a special place; it was the wildlife.

The squawks of parrots were part of the daily concert. Two pair of yellow heads came across from Punta Ycacos every morning, spent the day on our side as they foraged for fruits and seeds, then returned to their roosting site in the evening. A pair of osprey nested in a big tree behind our shack and their high altitude chirping added joy to the day. The frigatebirds soared so high they were often out of sight, but throwing out fish scraps would bring them down with the wind screaming through their wings. Pelicans in various stages of plumage went about their work catching small fish from the surface with their unique somersault dives. Occasionally one would alight on deck looking for a free meal.

My first introduction to a manatee had been as they passed by Orange Point on a calm night. Their breathing resembled a dolphins but in slow motion. Later we were accompanied by an individual who was so enamored with *Chance Along* that it followed us for a couple of miles as we sailed slowly by the mouth of the Rio Grande. But our encounters were rare and we considered each one a special event. So, I was excited when I saw that distinctive snout floating a few yards past *Chance Along*. The water is almost never clear in the bay, so I could not tell much about the creature attached to the nose, but it seemed to be drifting with the current. We watched it for quite some time until curiosity got the best of us, and Kirby and I hopped into the dinghy and rowed over. The nose didn't seem to know we were there and we assumed the owner was asleep. We slowly and quietly rowed back to *Chance Along*. As we were boarding one of the oars clattered into the bottom of the dinghy. Oops! We glanced back just as the nose disappeared and a dark back rolled above the surface like a sea serpent; the broad tail hung in the air for a brief second and whoosh, the manatee was gone.

Other than an occasional bird, mosquitoes, sand flies and deer flies ("doctor flies" in Belize, since they give injections), I had never expected that some of the wildlife might want to come aboard. It was with considerable surprise that we found a *woala* (boa constrictor), early one morning, wrapped around the bobstay. It wasn't big enough to be alarming, but still, this animal wasn't someone I would have invited to visit. We were anchored in mid-bay to get away from the shore insects (aforementioned); the snake apparently became tired of swimming and found a convenient place to rest.

Kirby took the boat hook and gently prodded it off into the water. It continued its journey gaining shore near our landing. Kirby's only comment, "If it has taken up residence in my shop I will have to prod it again." I was more concerned that the snake could have actually gained the deck from the bobstay. I really wouldn't have wanted to meet it in the forepeak.

It was the occasional visit from the large bottlenose that made us clap our hands in delight as they came to investigate *Chance Along*'s rounded bottom. With no bow wave to surf on, they rarely stayed long but would circle the bay scouting for dinner, often frolicking as they went. But in the season when the mullet came in large schools, the dolphins would stay the night. Frenzied mullet roiled the waters of the bay with the sound of a boiling cauldron, and the dolphins slapped their tails with force on the water and gorged. We would be thankful during those sleepless nights that we had the opportunity to witness this wilderness feast.

A pod of dolphins visited daily. They looked like bottlenose but were smaller and slightly darker in color, and unlike the bottlenose, they took little interest in *Chance Along*. They would come in the early part of the day, and while feeding and playing, circle the bay.

We were coming in on a windy afternoon, dousing sails and getting ready to anchor when, a hundred yards to windward, I noticed a large flock of frigates gathering over a turbulent area of the sea. I climbed up into the rigging with the binoculars and watched the commotion. A circle of dolphins surrounded another protectively, as it thrashed. Suddenly a dolphin reared up, two thirds of her body out of the water, and then fell back. Then again she was up on her tail, striking out with her nose at the close-circling birds. I could see a pink blob in the water that seemed to be attracting them. The birds continued to circle, trying to come down and the dolphin kept driving them away.

I had done enough reading about dolphin behavior to know what was taking place; I was witnessing a birthing. What the literature didn't tell was the possible harassment by other wildlife. The frigates must have been scavenging the afterbirth. The whole scene dissolved by the time we had anchored; I was left to wonder why the pod had come into the bay. Had the proximity of humans offered protection? And what about the dolphin infant, would it return again and again because this was its birth place? Despite the many questions the episode triggered, I felt privileged to have witnessed this special and intimate occurrence, one that made me feel a part of this place in a way I had not before.

When describing some of the events we have witnessed on the water, I am occasionally met with disbelief by some biologists who find it difficult to accept the observations of non-academic people. It is our slow pace of travel that allows our frequent sightings and gives us the time to make thorough examinations. Also varying, is the perspective of the viewer. We were beginning to feel we were no longer just passing through this watery world as observers; we had become members and we were keenly interested in learning more about our fellow creatures.

29

~~~

LIKE A LADY

There is no getting around it, woodturning is a dirty business—chips flying all over and dust coating everything in sight. When we first started the KirbyKraft business, it was set up in our one-room house, and Tina put up with it in the kitchen/bedroom until the barn was converted into a shop. She claimed the bread had a lot more substance during that period, being fortified with rosewood powder. But she drew the line at having dust drifting into the innumerable nooks and crannies on the boat. Yet, lathing aboard was necessary if we wanted to have mobility and money.

Though I had modified my big lathe to fit inside the aft cabin, my work aboard was limited to the open-to-all-weather aft deck where the breeze would carry the dust overboard. We made a trip back to Orange Point specifically to solve the problem. Tina sewed up some big panels of brown cotton to make a very large bag. I fastened strips of Velcro around the inside combings of the 4 by 6-foot aft cabin, and the bag sides were attached. My tools and I would be inside. Above the bag the ports and companionway remained open to the outside. Bear immediately jumped in, made a few circles and lay down, having no doubt this nest was made especially for him.

CHANCE ALONG

We spent the next morning loading tools, the generator, turning blanks, fuel, water, and supplies. For the first time since we had set up for our stateside trip in the old bus, we felt our business was mobile and looked forward to the freedom it would afford. Without a specific destination we planned to work our way up the coast and test our skills at being sea gypsies. The breeze came up, and I moved *Chance Along* around the point and into the bight. I tied Bear to the deck box so he wouldn't follow me ashore, instructed him to guard the boat, and rowed back.

After lunch Tina walked to town to get more sandpaper, and I finished the last of the turning blanks we would carry along. It had been a long, tiring day, but we were excited about the upcoming trip as we shoved off from the landing. When *Chance Along* came into view, Tina's face was suddenly stricken. I turned my head to see what she was looking at, and even in the waning light I knew he was dead. His body hung motionless over the side of the boat, his tail just touching the water. With us, Bear had finally found love, but he had never overcome his fear of abandonment. Whenever he sensed a threat to his source of affection, he went wild. He must have deduced that we were leaving on a bigger-than-usual trip and was afraid he would be left behind. In a frenzy he had dragged the deck box close enough to jump over the rail.

Amid the pain, we each blamed ourselves. I knew I should have tied him more securely, but Tina, tears streaming down her face, insisted it was her mistake in the beginning. "Our lives are too helter-skelter for a dog!"

Neither of us slept well, and as if mirroring our moods, the morning dawned overcast and squally. After giving Bear last rites, we re-boarded and got under way. We lost visibility off the Rio Grande and anchored rather than taking the risk of grounding in the narrow passage. In backing down on the anchor, I wrapped the trolling line, which should have been taken in, around the propeller and had to dive overboard to recover it. Sea travel doesn't allow for wandering minds and emotional instability—we vowed to get ourselves together.

Anchored in New Haven, we tried Tina's dust collector, and it worked great. A small fan pushed the finest dust out the companionway, and everything heavier settled around my feet. At the end of my turning session, I brushed down the sides of the bag, slipped it out from under the legs of the lathe table, and lifted the whole thing out. Now the gypsy wagon was ready to roll, and *Chance Along* was tugging at the bit like any good horse should. We were particularly excited because at last we were going to test the functionality of the top mast.

A few days before, Diana had sailed into New Haven on *Enchilada*. "That headsail has jammed on me for the last time," she said in exasperation. "I nearly wrecked before I could get it down!" She was strong for her size—she had to be to sail-singlehandedly—but her furling jib jammed when she was entering harbor and strength alone couldn't solve the problem. She wanted that sail off her boat and now! That's how we got our first main stays'l. The timing was perfect.

First light the next morning found a flotilla leaving New Haven. For an isolated harbor it was a quite an event. Four boats sailed together for a mile until reaching Punta Ycacos and then fanned out. Diana on *Enchilada* and Tina "Too Much" on *Baby Cake* turned south on a course that would take them to Livingston, Guatemala, where they would enter the Rio Dulce. It was a thirty-mile trip but they should have fair winds. Cosmic Bob, a friend from Cay Caulker, was headed for Placencia with his sloop. It was a twenty-five-mile trip and there would be headwinds much of the way. He turned northeast as soon as he cleared the point and started his motor to assist him.

We were bound for Placencia too, but were hoping to make it under sail alone. We continued to ride the morning land breeze to the east and an hour and a half later passed just north of East Snake Cay where we could see the metal tower for the new navigational light. Our new sail, built as a furling jib, was much too heavy, and it fit poorly, but it filled and there was a noticeable increase in speed. When the breeze shifted to the northeast and picked up, we dropped it and started tacking. Just before dark we entered Placencia harbor; it had been a rewarding day's sail. Later, Tina built a properly-fitting main stays'l of lightweight nylon. It was the final gown in *Chance Along*'s ensemble, and with all her sails she waltzes in the lightest of breezes.

Chance Along and her crew have had differences, but to my recollection she has always gotten her way. When it comes to compromise she stops short of being mule stubborn but could certainly be considered headstrong. A live-aboard sailboat is expected to be able to point within an angle of 60 degrees from the wind—a racing sloop would point significantly higher. Windward performance can be a weak point with schooners, so we were pleasantly surprised that in typical trade-wind conditions she would make 100 degree tacks, in other words, she was sailing 50 degrees off the wind. In a light breeze, it was altogether different.

On one of our first sails to New Haven, we had gone four or five miles and had another five to go when the land breeze faded. It was midmorning and hot. The dolphins had lost interest in us when we failed to produce a bow wave. I envied the frigatebirds above who made their vertical tacks on the slightest updraft and sailed on so effortlessly. The breeze had backed around to the east-northeast and was steady but light. Our sails were sheeted in fairly tightly, and though we moved at a reasonable speed back and forth across the channel, we made very little progress toward our windward destination. No matter how I trimmed, our tacks were never better than 120 degrees and sometimes worse. It was like the wind shifted in an adverse way every time I tacked. I complained to Tina about it and she responded, "Remember how Scott used to claim there are two winds?"

He was ten at the time and had built his own outrigger canoe with a bed-sheet sail. He had complained of the same phenomena while trying to tack around Orange Point. I had patiently explained to him that at any given time there could be different winds at different locations but only one wind at the same location. Later, I read that the wind the sails respond to, the *apparent* wind, is slightly different from the *real* wind since the motion of the boat through the water creates an airstream of its own; but a sailboat moves so slowly, the difference seemed like it would be insignificant.

On this particularly frustrating day, it finally dawned on me that with the wind blowing at only five or six knots, the boat's forward movement of two knots would change the apparent wind significantly. On the starboard tack it will effectively cause the wind to *back* (move counter-clockwise) a few degrees and on the port tack it will *veer* (move clockwise) the same amount. The result—a different wind on each tack! I mentally sent an apology to Scott for the misinformation. I eased the tiller I had been using to force *Chance Along* to do the impossible. She sighed in an I-tried-to tell-you sort of way, or maybe it was just the sound of her bow wave as she went to work.

Chance Along is not without vanity. By setting the trim tab to offset her slight weather helm and letting her steer herself, she can follow a light breeze more attentively than can most helmsmen. But while self-steering, she is sometimes seduced into following wind puffs that will leave her luffing like a jilted bride at the altar when the fickle breeze eases up. She is also proud of her lovely and generous transom. At anchor she will lie quietly pointing into the wind, but in those rare instances when a quick 180 degree shift occurs, she will first take her time running out the length of her anchor rode, then turn slowly, somewhat seductively, in a way that brings her transom across the eye of the wind. On occasion, we have had to use the mains'l alone to back out of a harbor, when sailing off the anchor in normal fashion would risk collision. *Chance Along*, getting an opportunity to show her shapely posterior, seems willing to sail in reverse all the way to Punta Gorda.

She is proud of her type and refuses to be handled in any other way than as a schooner. On a breezy afternoon soon after she was rigged, we were tacking up the inner channel of Port Honduras. The wind had increased steadily through the afternoon though the sky remained clear. In the gusts she would drop her rail down even with the water, and it was obvious we were carrying too much sail. As an expedient solution, I eased off the main sheet: effectively, we were using only the forward two sails. When I attempted to tack she ignored the helm for the first time, and I experienced the gut-wrenching knowledge that I no longer had control. Luckily there was enough sailing room to reverse my error without running aground. In essence I had tried to sail her like a sloop. Soon thereafter, we perfected our reefing technique and have sailed her as a schooner ever since. In a stiff afternoon breeze a reef in the fores'l and sometimes another in the main will let her point higher, sail faster and make her much more comfortable.

She has her way of getting attention when she thinks she is being ignored. Once we were invited to join a family outing in Placencia. As the afternoon breeze picked up, we loaded eight or ten young people for a short sail from the cove to the harbor. Most of the passengers were aft in the cockpit, and *Chance Along* was significantly out of trim. With her stern low and bow high, she refused to make her tack, and we had to ignominiously back her around to get on course. When she was launched, she floated parallel to Pete's designed waterline, and that is how she wants to be sailed. She will carry a heavy load without complaint, but her fore and aft trim must be kept, as if she knows when she looks her best.

As a special boat she deserves a special name, and in that regard, I am reminded of a conversation with our friend Pancho. His particular gift was teaching young people about bush skills, and our son was one of his students. Many people in Belize are known by their nicknames, and when we first met I asked him how he would like to be called. "My name is Francisco," he replied, "but my friends call me Pancho." After a moment he added, "But I am known as Panchito by those who love me." Since *Chance Along* has demonstrated her own unique personality, Tina and I have given her a nickname of her own. We can be heard to say as we leave the boat, "Take care of yourself, *Chancy*."

30

~~~

February-April 1991

SEA GYPSIES

Placencia was the first port-of-call for our new, mobile business. The tourism industry was growing quickly, and the season had been a good one. We made the rounds of the three gift shops we supplied, and each put in a small order. Back on board we set up the tools and went to work; just as quickly we found flaws in our system. Even with a new muffler, our generator made enough noise to violate the early morning quietness of the harbor, and we were sure the sound travelled ashore to the local residents. In the afternoon, when the harbor was active, there were plenty of competing sounds to drown out ours, but the sea breeze made the anchorage rolly and lathing became difficult.

We motored two miles south to the ship channel and on into the commercial port of Big Creek. There the waters were calm, and noise was not an issue; we went to work in earnest. The freighter, *Paxi Rex*, came in to take on a load of bananas. She had dumped some of her water ballast to get in through the shallow channel, and the tip of her propeller was clear of the water. It was fascinating to see her being maneuvered in such tight quarters—she only had fifty feet of clearance when she was turned. We were glad the tugs were doing all the work; the wash from her prop could have driven us into the mangroves.

We concentrated on our work and were very productive, but after a week in the confined anchorage we were ready to break out. We filled our water jugs at the commercial pier and motored back to Placencia. Our customers were impressed at how quickly we had filled their orders; we sold our week's production and most of the stock we had brought with us. But in doing so we had temporarily saturated the market. We were ready to move on to the next port—that was the beauty of being mobile! At last we were living the dream.

Sailors like to tell stories, either about the glorious trips with perfect winds and clear skies, or about the terrible storms they barely survived. I suppose I am guilty of doing the same, but in truth the large majority of our sailing experiences, the next three days for example, were neither of the above. A cold front was approaching and by midmorning of the following day, the wind was howling into the exposed south end of Placencia harbor. When she pitched, *Chance Along* was almost putting her bowsprit in the water. We hauled her anchor up and motored through the narrow northern cut and into the placid waters of the cove. But by late evening, the wind swung and exposed us to a northwest gale. Not wanting to play the game of musical anchorages, we retraced our course down to the ship channel but this time continued another mile south to anchor near Harvest Cay. It isn't a great anchorage, is not very deep and is tricky to get to, but it gives moderate protection from all quarters.

The next day was spent comfortably, doing boat chores, and during the night the front passed on and the wind moderated. Eager to be on our way, we motored back to Placencia and out through the northern cut, but now the breeze was too light and without sail power we couldn't punch through the residual swell. We re-anchored, and then tried to relax. It seemed time to determine why life suddenly had become so difficult.

We had no time commitments, so why were we pushing so hard? In truth, we had subconsciously set a schedule just because we were ready to go. We had to remind ourselves that our goal is to work with Nature; it is the most basic of requirements for those who travel by sail power. We ignore the elements at our own peril; still, when the conditions are favorable we must be prepared to take advantage of them. Ultimately it is Mother Nature who sets sailing schedules.

As if to reward our patience, the swell calmed down, and a mild northwest wind filled in during the night; we were underway by dawn. In late afternoon we sailed into the Blue Ground range and anchored in six fathoms. This group of mangrove cays is scattered but reefs between them provide moderate protection from every direction. We had the anchorage to ourselves until a 30-foot cutter arrived and anchored 100 yards away. Hal and Ellen, with their black Schipperke, rowed over for a visit. Having seen our flag, they had lots of questions about living in Belize, but also sailing experiences of their own to share. Both Tina and I gave undue attention to the little dog and during a lull in the conversation, Tina turned to me, her eyes welling, and whispered, "I sure miss Bear, don't you?"

They were very generous, and before we left in the morning, they brought us 60 feet of high-tensile anchor chain, a gimbaled, kerosene cabin lamp and a depth chart for the Bay Islands of Honduras. We gave them the last of our craft items—a rosewood bracelet and two serving bowls and, through our conversation, a view of our way of life.

Fifteen knots of wind on the beam, perfect for *Chance Along*, carried us the 26 miles to the Blue Fields range. A supper of two freshly-caught mackerel completed a wonderful day. The southeast "feeder" breeze, the low barometer, and the congregation of four fishing smacks were all indicators that another front was due. By midmorning a northwest gale was blowing. Though the

SALTWATER, SAILS, AND SUNSETS

wind howled through the rigging and only a small strip of land lay between us and the slamming waves, we felt comfy in our anchorage. Snugness aboard is a special sensation, perhaps like being in a nice warm cabin during a blizzard. It seems to be derived from feelings of security, and at the same time vulnerability, that are only experienced by those exposed to Nature's raw forces.

The next day the wind remained steady but not over 25 knots. We hoisted the foresail alone, sheeted it in tight and with the Perkins at a fast idle we motor-sailed the 13 miles to the Drowned Cays. The sea was rough but *Chance Along* easily threw the waves aside—I could imagine her commenting, "I can handle a lot more than you can, my dears." This extensive group of mangrove cays forms the eastern and north-eastern perimeter to the Belize City harbor. The *bogues* (inlets) provide protection from any wind but not from the myriad of sand flies that reside there—we anchored well offshore.

The Baron Bliss regatta was to be held the next day and we had hoped to attend. But the strong and cold (relatively speaking) wind continued and we knew many of the small boat events would be cancelled. The thought of the five mile beat to windward and the likelihood of spending the day and maybe the night in an exposed anchorage was not attractive. In our coastal cruising, predicting the conditions in which we will spend the night became as important as planning the trip itself. We settled in for a day of reading, writing and reflection as we listened to the race events on the radio.

CHANCE ALONG

Blow cold norther blow;
Your manner rude and chill
Instills the seas with wrath;
Of power, enjoy the thrill.

Though you hold me to my cove
I have lines to write and splice;
I've provisions, warmth, and love
And patience, your strength twice.

For bound by natural law
Your passion can't prevail;
When your awesome strength is spent
We humble raise our sail

And continue on the course
That we were on before,
Your era soon forgotten
Like wavelets on the shore.

Yes, we have found it best
To wait our chance along;
For a fair wind in our sails
And in our hearts a song.

KGS

When the trade winds again dominated the weather, we sailed through the narrow Porto Stuck and on toward Cay Caulker. The coastal waters north of Belize City are shallow, two fathoms or less, and with few rivers to feed them are usually clearer than those in the south. With no mountains on the mainland to add their thermal component, the breezes are more easterly and are often favorable for sailing both up and down this north-south reef line. Reading depths was much easier, but it was hard to relax while watching the bottom slide by so close under the keel. *Chance Along* loved it, and we were impressed with her speed now that she had a fair wind.

Cay Caulker is only a few hundred yards from the reef, and fishing was the primary industry, but a number of guest houses had been built and tourism was getting a start. Our friends, Jim and Dorothy, sold our craft items in their shop, but their main business was focused on Jim's passion for wildlife photography. *Seeing Is Belizing* was their logo, and they offered a lovely selection of postcards and prints. They were sailors as well and were generous in sharing their experiences with us. Their simplified lifestyle gave them time to pursue photography and, like us, to explore their relationship with Nature.

After a few conch *flitters* and some key lime pie from a snack shop, we sailed back south a few miles to Cay Chapel and entered the marina. The cay is privately owned, has its own airstrip, and in 1991 had a resort on the beach in the motif of a 1960's motel. The marina had space for about a dozen boats, and we moored *Chance Along* in one of the slips—the first time she had been tethered to anything but an anchor line. We had electricity and pressurized water available, and though we had no built-in systems, an extension cord could be run directly to the lathe. Previously, the use of any electrical tool, whether aboard or at Orange Point, was preceded by starting a generator. Being able to activate the lathe with the mere flip of a switch was something akin to magic.

Schmitty's shop was adjacent to the marina; sprouting out of its roof was a forest of antennas that supported his amateur radio hobby. His gruff demeanor belied a generous heart and we got along well. He had come to Belize several decades earlier and had found his niche as head of maintenance on the cay. His was a novel approach to job security. It was said he had gone through all the refrigeration units when he first arrived, ripping out parts he claimed were not necessary, and replaced them with a few secret gadgets of his own devising. From then on he was the only one who could keep them working.

The dockage fees began the moment we tied up, and our lathing commenced shortly thereafter. The work went quickly with no anchors or sails to tend, no rolling to compensate for and, blessedly, no generator noise. In a few days we had filled Dorothy's order and were building up our stock again. Once or twice a week, our friend, Robert, on the rebuilt Chesapeake buy-boat, *Winnie Estelle,* brought a charter group from San Pedro to visit the island and we usually sold a few items to them. With the little lathe set up in the cockpit, I turned custom-fitted bangles for the tourists as they watched from the dock. When our turning blanks ran low, we called Carlos, and he sent more on the airplane that landed only a few dozen yards from the marina.

What a luxurious life! Whenever we wanted, we could stroll across the cay and buy cold soft-drinks. There was live music on Saturday nights and beach volleyball on Sundays. Good snorkeling and fishing sites were nearby, and we could hitch a ride on the resort's boat to re-provision in Belize City. At night the balmy sea breeze blew, and our decks glistened with palm-shattered moonlight. It was a romantic setting, and we responded as if we were newlyweds.

Yet, even though we were in an environment designed for recreation, our need to continue working reminded us that we were *not* tourists. At meal times, the island guests sat down to sumptuous meals prepared by the professional staff at the restaurant. We also ate wholesome and delicious meals but only after Tina had labored in the galley to prepare them. The guests left in the mornings for a day of snorkeling, diving or fishing while I submerged into the aft cabin for a day of wood turning.

It gave us an appreciation for the adjustment that many Belizeans must make to adapt to the tourism industry and why resentment can easily surface. An independent fisherman sets his own schedule based on the phase of the moon, the tides, the weather and his market. His success or failure depends heavily on the decisions he makes—he is his own man. A fishing guide must have his own set of skills, but his schedule and destination will be determined mainly by his clients. He may have a larger and more assured income, but he will have to experience the class distinction inherent to the industry: there are those who receive a service and there are those who provide it.

Occasionally it chafed to be a provider, but overall our work was satisfying. Rosewood is a renewable resource, and we were growing it at Orange Point faster than we were using it. We had a unique, high-quality product that not only provided the income to support a way of life that we enjoyed, it served us as a creative outlet.

It was an advantage to come from the same culture as the customers and to have some of the same tastes. If I shaped the turnings so they were pleasing to my eye, the potential buyers found them attractive too. Sharing the same culture was a major advantage throughout the tourism industry: in selecting a setting and a design for guest cottages, in making the grounds attractive, in choosing enjoyable entertainment and providing services and products. But perhaps even more important was the fact that the culture we had come from had taught us that providing good service was something to be proud of.

After Easter, when the tourist season slowed down, so did our sales. We had to face up to some financial realities. We were paying a lot for the convenience of the marina— much more than the expense of operating a small generator. We had always needed to supplement our turning income in the off season by work, such as furniture making, that required a land base for large stationary tools. In addition, *Chance Along* would need to be hauled out again in a few months. As pleasant as our Cay Chapel life was, it alone was not going to provide the income we needed.

Still, we had a good stock of craft items, a little money in our pockets and a beautiful sailing breeze. We cast off our lines, motored out into the channel and raised sail. We basked in the luxury of sailing north without beating into wind and waves. We could understand why there were so many working sailboats in these northern waters. Traveling so close to the reef, the waves were small, and the mild wind on the beam was a sailor's dream come true.

We ran along Ambergris Cay with its miles of white-sand beaches to port and the reef only a few hundred yards to starboard. The shallow waters were crystal clear and varied in color from dark green, where the bottom was grassy, to aqua where it was sand. Out closer to the reef, the coral patches appeared brownish-yellow. A white, lacy surf-line marked the reef itself and beyond it was the dark blue of deep water. It was here we had snorkeled for the first time twenty years earlier, and we knew that as spectacular as the colors were above the surface, they couldn't compare with those below.

We had set up a schedule to make contact with Christie every two weeks. We would search out a public telephone wherever we found ourselves, and she would go to the phone office in Punta Gorda. On that day she had alarming news—she and Carlos had been offered their old jobs back—they planned to leave for Dallas in ten days' time. We knew they had used all their savings to start their house and were having a hard time finding the money to finish it, still the news came as a shock; it would have a big effect on us since Orange Point couldn't be left unattended. In a short time our possessions would start to "walk away" and the jungle would gradually take back the clearing we had wrestled from it. I thought back to Sid's words, "If you really want a life on the water, you will get rid of your property at Orange Point." We hadn't heeded that advice and now we must return.

In the morning, I mentally cast off my sailor suit and put on the cloak of Kirby Kraft, the super salesman. Though occupancy had already dropped at Ramón's resort, I was able to convince the gift shop to restock for the fall, and we sold almost everything we had. With the galley provisioned and our water and fuel jugs full, we raised sail and headed south. Orange Point's magnetism had drawn us to it in the beginning, now it was pulling us back again. We tried to set our reluctance aside and summon the faith that there was purpose in this change of direction.

31

~~~

June 1991—November 1992

OPPORTUNITY KNOCKS

Within a few weeks of our return to Orange Point, Kirby came from Punta Gorda looking elated. "Do you think we can get the boat cleaned up and ready to sail by Saturday?"

"Why?" I asked warily. I was just getting settled into shore life in Christie's house.

"Brian and Anne want us to take them out for a day trip. I know it is a bit of work to get *Chance Along* ready, but it would be nice to go sailing, and we'd get paid for it. It's a chance to see what chartering would be like."

Brian and Anne had recently set up a small plant in nearby Forest Home to refine dolomite for the agricultural industry, and we had visited with them several times. Despite having emphatically said I would *never* consider sharing my little domain with strangers, it would be very mean-spirited to say no. "I'm game, but a little nervous. They seem like really nice people, and I think they would be easy to accommodate. So . . . okay." A few days later we dropped anchor near the Texaco pier and Kirby rowed in to pick them up. Brian had a cooler of beer and soft drinks that he hefted onto the deck. Anne had a big picnic basket of Danish snacks. Her nephews, Christopher and Neils, were curious about every aspect of the schooner. Back in Denmark their family kept boats.

It was a lovely day. We motored the seven miles out to Moho Cay where I served a lunch of chicken/rice salad, barbequed beans and fresh-baked, English muffins. Our guests snorkeled around the coral heads and explored the beach of the tiny cay. The sea breeze picked up by mid-afternoon, and we raised our sails for the easy run back. After anchoring, Kirby rowed everyone into the dock while I coiled lines, put fenders away, and prepared for the last couple miles to Yankee Doodle Bight.

"Well, that wasn't too bad," Kirby watched to see that the mainsail didn't jibe.

"Yes, it went better than I expected. They seemed to really enjoy being aboard, and Anne was appreciative of our effort."

"Yes, very!" Anne had not quibbled about price at all. Her check was down on the cabin table.

Looking closely into my face he asked, "Would you do it again?"

"Hmm, yes, I think I would, but not too often. It is fun in its way, but the responsibility of people's safety is stressful, and it's a challenge to carry on a conversation with several people and still be attentive to the boat."

"But we will learn; it will diversify our income." He carefully set the trim tab and brought the mains'l over as we rounded Orange Point and entered the narrow channel leading to the bight. To judge his distance from shore, he glanced over at the tips of the VOA towers showing just above the trees. "You know, for as much anguish as those damned things have caused me, they do make good navigational aids."

Opportunity was splashing us in the face. Chartering was another option for making a living, and like the wood turning, we could do it anywhere. But if we wanted to offer charter service to the general public we would have to finish the interior. We couldn't have pigtail buckets tumbling about with guests on board. Now, while we weren't living aboard and had the use of a wood shop, would be a good time to do the work.

My three-year experience onboard had given me a good idea of what I wanted for a permanent cabin layout. Kirby's priorities were somewhat different since he had to consider the construction complexities and the materials available. As we had done so many times before, we each compromised a bit. The effort of working it out together brought a much more satisfactory solution than either of us had devised on our own.

The work progressed slowly for there was much time spent coming and going in the dinghy. Materials and tools had to be rowed the half mile down to the anchorage and the return trip was often against the sea breeze. I gave the whole interior a couple coats of paint while Kirby was making patterns for the permanent parts and preparing the stock.

Kirby cut, fitted and fastened; I followed behind, filling, sanding, staining, painting or varnishing. The raised panels used for settee backs, engine, and galley doors were of mahogany, and the galley counter and dinette table were of rosewood. Spindled rails kept the shelved items in place. These pieces, along with the cabin-top beams, the carlin trim, and cabin sole were varnished, and the other surfaces were painted off-white. I was happy with the cheery but elegant effect that resulted.

Finally, our living area had two comfortable bunks, three-quarter size (by folding down the settee back and pulling out a specially-shaped, foam mattress), a compact galley with stainless steel sink and stove to starboard, and a small two-person dinette to port, plus lots of storage incorporated under, around and behind each unit. The details included paneled doors and, for ventilation, dolphin-shaped cut-outs. The placement of each unit gave a symmetrical aspect to the whole cabin. Friends, John and Bonny aboard *Phalcor*, completed our charter needs from their salvage collection—a used marine head. With new curtains and cushion covers to set it all off, we had a comfortable and homey living area. I was so pleased!

All the rowing with the charter and the back and forth to *Chance Along,* let us know we needed a new dinghy with better design characteristics and more carrying capacity. *Oardeal* did the job, but its basic plan emphasized amateur building and economy of materials rather than function; it rowed poorly and sailed even worse. I looked at many dinghy designs and one in particular, Joel White's Nutshell, attracted my attention. It was nice to look at, was simply rigged, and received raves for its sailing and rowing abilities. Unfortunately, it was to be built of marine plywood which was not available in Belize. Still, Kirby was confident that he could design a similar one that would allow construction from locally-available materials.

Needing a space to build, we put all of Christie's old hens into canning jars, cleaned the coop and started building. I got out the treadle Singer and made a sail from hunting-vest cloth brother Russ had gotten at auction. Six weeks later we launched *Tag Along*. She was all we could ask for in her ease of rowing and her amazing stability and load-carrying capacity. She was a delight to sail and was not likely to get accidentally run over with her day-glow-orange sail!

After being out on the water for several years, I absorbed the essence of the forest like a sponge, taking the greenness into my cells. I renewed my relationship with the creatures I had lived with for so many years. It was like coming home—the forest reached out and enfolded me and gave me a sense of security.

I realized that if land clearing continued as it had on the VOA property, the present generation of children might never experience the wonders of a tropical forest. I decided to begin a project of my own. During several weeks of the dry season, I hacked my way through our property until I found some interesting sites, and with hired help, cut trails to link them. I typed up a little guidebook to explain the significance of each site: the ants living in the thorn of the cockspur tree demonstrated a symbiotic relationship; the strangler fig represented the intense competition for sunlight; the bay leaf and cohune palms are materials used for thatching, and a smaller palm make useful brooms. Many of the hard wood trees make good lumber, and there are many parts of the plants, trees, and shrubs used for medicine.

I sent invitations to the primary school teachers to bring out small groups of students. They were encouraging, for they also realized that many of the children had never been out of the town limits. The teachers remembered going out to the forest to gather firewood and to make plantations with their parents or grandparents and considered such experiences valuable.

I even imagined how Christie and Carlos could, on their return, make a little income with the nature trail by making it available to adventurous tourists. Kirby carved a sign for the property entrance, and from that time on we have referred to the place as Falcon Forest. We chose the laughing falcon as a totem to keep us from taking our endeavors too seriously. It hunts quietly in the forest and is rarely seen to alight. When it chooses to voice its ribald laugh, we can't help but think it is laughing at mankind's follies.

As long as I was busy, I could ignore the restlessness. For the first year ashore we had been busy with the boat interior, the dinghy and the nature trail. In addition we had to maintain the property and buildings, and of course, make our living with the craft business. But as our projects were completed and I had more free time, the feeling increased. I noticed it most when I rowed down to the bight to check on *Chance Along*. I wanted to raise the sails, haul the anchor and go! The forest that had felt so welcoming a few months ago was now making me feel hemmed in. I had enjoyed its green melody but now I missed the blue song of the sea.

After eighteen months ashore, serendipity offered us a way back to our water life. Carlos's uncle, Emanuel, had lived most of his adult life on Amado Creek, a tributary to the Moho River, which enters the sea two miles south of Orange Point. He lived alone—his closest neighbor several miles away. He planted corn and beans for himself and hewed wooden beams for his source of cash. For a man in his middle sixties, he was in remarkably good physical condition, but a series of incidents had made him uneasy, and he decided he couldn't continue to live in such isolation. After a telephone discussion with Carlos, we offered him a job at Orange Point as caretaker.

Kirby and I sat on the porch steps, coffee cups in hand, "Can you believe how little *Tio* (uncle) gets by with?" I paused. "He makes my efforts at simplicity a mockery." He had arrived that morning with all his possessions in his narrow sixteen-foot dory.

Kirby shook his head, "It is amazing. On the other hand, it seems the clutter culture we come from won't loosen its grip on us. For a two-week trip we load *Chance Along* with several times the amount of things he arrived with. And of course, we leave most of our stuff here at Orange Point."

I often feel wasteful as well as handicapped by so many things. It would feel satisfying to be burdened only by a spoon, a cup, a bowl and a pot, but I doubt I can ever be so frugal. My pleasures in the kitchen and galley and with the sewing machine and typewriter require many items, and all of them have to be stored and maintained.

Tio came to sit with us. Spanish was his first language, but he spoke a lovely, colonial English, and his manners were those of a gentleman of a past era. "Thank you, Mister. Thank you, Misses, for the tea (meal). I will go this afternoon to buy provisions and prepare my household. I will be happy to keep the property secure for you and for Carlos."

Kirby leaned closer to speak into his good ear, "Tio, how did you get home after your fall?"

"I had been carrying a bag of corn and when I fell my knee was out of place. I cut a forked stick, stuck it in the ground, put my foot in it and pulled. It popped back into place, but the pain was plentiful, and I had a long way to walk. I had to leave my corn in the bush; I fed the animals! That is a good joke. It is all right. That is life. Now I am here. It is good."

32

~~~

May 1993—May 1995

GETTING A LITTLE DINGHY

It was probably my imagination, but *Chance Along* seemed livelier with a new dinghy in her davits and a proper interior layout. I felt pretty frisky myself—aboard again after having lived ashore for a year and a half. Yet, we had made good use of our time. In addition to our boat improvements, Tina's nature trail had been a success. The delight the students and teachers received from the experience was reward enough for the hard work, and we had learned a lot more about our little forest from Tio as he shared his knowledge of medicinal plants.

About ten minutes after we dropped anchor in New Haven, Tina had the sail on the dinghy and was underway. The bay was a perfect environment for *Tag Along,* a good breeze and fairly smooth water, and we found sailing the dinghy an enjoyable way to improve our skills. Now Tina had *wheels,* or more appropriately *wings,* of her own when I took *Oardeal* ashore to do my lathing. I could hardly wait to put *Tag* to work trolling a lure.

I had really enjoyed building her, and Tina found pleasure in shaping and sewing up the sail. Compared to the complexities of building the schooner, the dinghy construction was fairly simple, but there was a lot of

SALTWATER, SAILS, AND SUNSETS

satisfaction in being able to create a sailing vessel in only a few weeks' time. We hoped to further broaden our earning base by selling dinghies to some of the cruising people. First we would need to locate a sawyer to cut thin, mahogany planks, but the most pressing issue was having enough working space at New Haven.

During the next several trips to Orange Point, we took advantage of *Chance Along's* workboat heritage: her wide decks and her load-carrying capability. We were also glad for her sturdy cap rails and the fact we could touch up the scrapes with a few coats of enamel instead of eight coats of varnish. We carried all the framing materials for a 14 by 18-foot shed, the corrugated metal to roof it, and the concrete materials to build footings. Though there may have been a cruising yachtsman or two who shuddered at the misuse of our beautiful schooner, the designer would have approved, having freighted with his own boat.

It was a simple structure, and it went up quickly. Ron gave us a hand when the task required more muscle. The roof was steeply pitched to allow space for lumber storage. The walls were framed but not sided; the ground would have to serve as a floor until we had more lumber. Ventilation would be no problem and we hung tarps that could be rolled down for rain protection. Along one wall was a work bench with a slot cut in it where my circular saw could be mounted to serve as a table saw. Hand tools, electric and mechanical, were adequate for the construction. Tools and supplies were kept in the old shack where I did my lathing. It wasn't fancy, but it was economical, kept us out of the rain, and it provided a good-sized working area.

We made a price list for the "New Haven Dinghy" and offered it in three sizes: eight, ten and twelve feet. We also offered the eight-foot Oardeal and a sixteen-foot canoe, both made from construction plywood. Though we preferred tholepins for our own dinghy, our commercial boats had shiny bronze oarlocks. We planned to promote our new

~ 263 ~

products by sailing around each harbor, and we considered writing an ad on the sail, something like a floating version of the sandwich board, but decided that the orange sail should attract enough attention on its own.

On our next trip up the coast, we received our first order. We were anchored on the west side of Cay Caulker and had delivered rosewood to Dorothy. She told us about the new house they were constructing at the southern tip of the cay. Jim said they were building on a limited budget but already had a garbage disposal—two medium-sized crocodiles that came with the place.

We had just arrived back aboard when Diana rowed over from *Enchilada*. She had seen us sailing back and forth from the dock. "I just have to have a dinghy I can sail. Could you make me one like yours but a little smaller?" It was perfect timing for us. The tourist season was winding down and we would have the summer months to build it. We already had the materials on hand, having ordered extra when we built *Tag*. We wrote up an agreement and took her deposit.

We had the new boat finished when Diana arrived in the fall. She flitted around like a sandpiper during the launch ceremony where she christened her new boat *Salsa*. It was apparent she got a lot of joy sailing her new dinghy and we received nearly as much just watching. One afternoon she and a friend sailed down to Wild Cane Cay, farther away than we had been in *Tag*, and tacked back against a stiff sea breeze.

Unfortunately, we overestimated the appeal of the sailing dinghies to cruising people. They enjoyed seeing us sail but were reluctant to give up the speed of the ubiquitous, motor-driven inflatable. We began to realize that wanting to live on a sailboat and sailing just for pleasure are two different things. Diana was the exception not the rule.

Most of our KirbyKraft customers were the owners of seaside resorts, and we started offering our little boats as a new item. We built another little eight-footer on speculation and showed it to a couple resorts on the Placencia peninsula. The first place already had plastic sailboats and kayaks to entertain their guests, but the owner of the second was a wood lover. Though his main lodge was concrete, he had used timber throughout in very imaginative and lovely ways. He took one look at this little boat, bronze fittings shining, the solid mahogany spars and sheer strake glowing under several coats of varnish, and he fell in love. "I suppose it is selfish," he said, "but I am going to keep it for my personal use." I glanced at this gentle giant and at the little dinghy. I really wanted the sale, but my conscience was poking me with the end of its oar.

"I could build you a bigger one that might be more suitable," I offered.

"No, this is the boat I want," he said firmly.

On our next trip to Placencia we delivered his rosewood order for the fall season. I was amazed to find that our dinghy, looking brand new, was featured as the center piece in the lobby, as if it were a sculpture. He explained, "I took it out for the first time on a choppy afternoon. It was fun rowing around, and I decided to try sailing. I didn't even get the sail up when a wave came over the side and I swamped. I decided it makes a better art piece and now all my guests can enjoy it."

We made our biggest sale to Dave. He was building a resort just west of Placencia. His project was separated from the village proper by a narrow canal, and it could only be accessed by water. He decided to make a virtue of this feature and ordered an Oardeal to go with each of his four rooms. In addition he wanted a canoe and a ten-foot sailing dinghy for general use. We were elated—along with our normal rosewood orders we had enough work for a year.

KirbyKraft, New Haven branch, went into production. Materials were purchased in quantity, and patterns were made so the parts for all the Oardeals could be cut at one time. Suddenly our new shop was too small; it looked like I imagined a violin maker's shop might. Dinghies hanging from the ceiling joists gave working area below, but space was a small issue compared to the insects.

Each of the winter cold fronts create certain conditions that bring out the sand flies in clouds. Just being ashore was unbearable without trying to get anything accomplished and working right at ground level didn't help. The best solution was to burn coconut husks. They were put to smolder in a metal bucket that could be positioned so the smoke would envelop the victim. It made it hard to breathe, difficult to see, and was probably carcinogenic, but it gave relief from the biting flies. When fully clothed, rubber-booted and scarfed, I could manage to operate at about half my normal efficiency. A certain amount of time was lost because it was periodically necessary to take a break for a good scream. In addition, Tina wouldn't let me into the cabin with my smoky clothes.

I had just climbed aboard after a rough day.

"That smell is terrible!" she said.

"I am planning on condensing the smoke, bottling it, and selling it as a man's cologne," I told her. "I will call it 'Husk'. Doesn't that sound virile? I'm sure it will turn the women on."

"Forget it," she said. "Take off your clothes!"

"See," I shouted gleefully, "it works!"

Mike greeted us at his bar in Placencia, "You looked like some kind of a carnival when you sailed in." We certainly hadn't appeared like the average cruiser, and if a cruiser at all, we looked like one who was paranoid about sinking—we had five dinghies! *Tag*, white with blue trim, was in her normal place in the davits. A yellow Oardeal was on deck leaning against the port side of the main cabin, a green one was opposite on the starboard side, and two more were trailing astern—one pink, one blue; the dinghies were color-coordinated to match the cabañas they would serve. On our previous trip we had delivered a canoe and a ten-foot sailing dinghy.

At the same time, Mike had given us tee shirts that advertised his Dockside Bar and I noticed him glance to see if we were wearing them. Tina picked up on his disappointment, and said, "Today we are advertising *our* new product line," and she turned to let him read the back of her shirt.

Old Sailors Never Die
They Just Get
A Little Dinghy
(From KirbyKraft)

33

~~~

May 1993—May 1995.......

CHANCY SHARING

In late afternoon, the thunderheads had built up over the Maya Mountains to the west and across the bay in Guatemala and Honduras. After dark, the horizon was a panoramic brilliance as the towering cloud masses tried to outshine each other with internal heat lightning. The grumbling symphony was occasionally accented by the cymbal crash of a bolt as it found its target. In the middle of the night, the storm whipped down on us under full throttle. These night storms could reach 60 knots for short periods of time—conditions that break anchor lines and drive boats ashore.

The lightning lit up the scene in dazzling bursts, the kind that record pink flashes on your retina even with your eyes closed. The thunder rumbled and pounded until the water vibrated. Even I, who had experienced many of these storms, could appreciate this one's almost malevolent character. The schooner's hull was saturated in tension—the fear palpable. Though the wind was howling, we were protected in our mangrove anchorage, and our main fear was not for the boat, but for the effect the storm was having on our guests. I questioned our judgment in accepting a charter at this time of year.

We had come down from the cays in the early morning and picked up our party of four at the Texaco dock. In prior correspondence, this family, Mom, Dad, son aged 12 and a friend also 12, had explained that they could only come in July, the height of the rainy season. I had tried to impress on them that the weather could be quite unpredictable and sometimes violent that month. They were looking for an adventure and felt they could handle it. We had agreed, with reservations.

Stopping at Moho Cay to swim and snorkel we ate a late picnic lunch and then continued on to our anchorage. We fed them dinner, discussed a plan for the week's activities and the safety rules. We squeezed the boys into a make-shift "V" berth in the forepeak and tucked the parents into the main cabin bunks. Kirby and I slept in the aft cabin where the transom rail was handy in the night, thus leaving the head exclusively for the guests.

Anticipating the storm, we slept lightly. As soon as we felt the wind shift we were on deck taking down the awning and wind scoop; Kirby let out a little more anchor line. I was used to getting up during these storms to check whether we were dragging and then to read until the storm passed. This night I had to stay in my bunk where I tossed and turned while thinking how great it would be to have a cup of tea. It abated about three o'clock, the tension oozed away, and there was silence aboard until dawn. Bodies emerged from below to greet a beautiful tropical morning; the vividly blue sky was breath-taking, the mangroves and distant hills vibrantly clear in their various hues of green, and sparkling, dancing water surrounded us.

The faces were haggard; the night's memories lurked behind glazed eyes. Over breakfast I told them it would be no problem for us if they wanted to return to shore to finish their vacation with mainland activities. "I understand that this experience might be more than you bargained for." We left them to consider while we cleaned up breakfast, did boat chores, and made ready to get underway. When I asked which direction we should head, the mother spoke for them, "We have decided to continue."

One of the boys chimed in, "If we survived last night, we can survive anything!" We could sense his feeling of achievement, having lived through a fine sample of Nature's fury. *That's the spirit*, I thought, *welcome to the real world!*

The days were fairly clear, and we had no more heavy night storms while they were aboard. The trip went smoothly. We showed them the wonders of the mangrove cays and explored a Mayan site. We picked fruit and drank coconut water, threw the cast net for bait and ate fresh-caught fish. The water was clear enough to have good snorkeling in the Snake Cays, and using reference books, the sea creatures were identified. On our slow sail to Placencia we were entertained by the biggest pod of bottlenose we had ever seen. They frolicked around the boat for an hour or more.

Still, it was a challenge to keep the boys entertained. When the dolphins came to play, when the frigates soared, or the fish took the hook, it was Kirby and I who led the group in excitement. We were the ones who felt contentment as we furled the sails after a good passage. Snorkeling kept their attention the longest, but in the storytelling afterward, they made comparisons with what they had seen in nature programs on TV. They hadn't petted the dolphins, seen them mating, nor witnessed an encounter with a shark. That's the problem when you use Nature as a source of entertainment for guests; sometimes they find it boring and other times it will scare their pants off.

After five days, we returned them to Punta Gorda to meet their flight home. They assured us it had been a memorable experience. We hoped so because we had given them everything we had to offer. In exhaustion, we got a few supplies and headed back to the cays and our anchorage. In the evening, we mulled over the experience—

had their expectations been met, and were we compensated adequately for what we had given? In truth, we expected more than just the dollars; we were not just providing a service—we were sharing our life.

"Maybe we shouldn't advertise overnight charters anymore," Kirby said. "We can consider those who come to us by word-of-mouth, but I don't want to jade our experiences by selling them to just any comer." I sighed in relief; he had whittled away the superfluous. He had picked up on the unease I was feeling at sharing what to me were nearly sacred places—personal and private. Kirby and I were in tune, not just with our surroundings, but with each other.

Our day charters were more successful, in part, because we could be more selective about the weather, and we could stick to one or two destinations. *Chance Along*'s working sounds and easy motion, when combined with a clear sky and a gentle, balmy breeze, could break down almost anyone's indifference. Sometimes, we were rewarded in ways we never expected.

We had been doing day trips out of Placencia during the height of the tourist season, and our agent had lined up a family of five. Kirby picked them up with *Tag* at the Shell dock, and as they boarded, it was apparent that the youngest child, about 13, was blind. We motor sailed against a light easterly breeze and reached Scipio Cay by midday. Our concerns about Danny's safety faded as his siblings, in their middle teens, guided him around the boat, describing it in detail as they went. Soon he was following them up the ratlines and leaping off into the water. The three teenagers snorkeled as a team, stopping occasionally to discuss what they were seeing. Danny was as excited as the others.

The breeze picked up in the afternoon and we started our sail back. The older kids had the chance to steer, and neither could get used to pushing the tiller right to go left and vice versa. Kirby faced Danny forward, put the tiller in his hand and asked him to feel where the wind was on his face. He had him turn the boat a little each way and return to the original course. Danny really put his mind to it, and aided by his exceptionally keen senses, he could soon keep the course better than either of his siblings! His face glowed.

We had chartered with Lee several times but this one was of longer duration. Lee was researching the birds of Belize for his field guide and asked us to carry him through the southern cays—all of them—to do a survey. His colleague, Martin, also an avid birder, would be joining us. These men were serious about their research and wanted to examine "every scrap of soil out there." They planned to leave no stone unturned and no tern unsighted.

From New Haven we travelled to the Snake Cays and then out to the southern end of the reef twenty miles away. During the next week, we worked our way north another thirty miles to Gladden Cay and finally back west to

Placencia. We stopped at each sand spit and cay to make a quick census and to look for nesting sites.

It was a workout for everyone. I tried to have breakfast finished by the time we had enough visibility to travel. Lunch and dinner varied from snacks to a full meal depending on the sea conditions and comfort of our anchorage. Lee and Martin took turns rowing to make their innumerable landings while Kirby and I managed *Chance Along*, sometimes anchoring and other times standing offshore until they rejoined us.

It was a tired crew that sailed into Placencia but a satisfied one too. Lee and Martin had found several nesting sites, and the information they had gathered would be incorporated in the new book. Not only had we learned a lot about the creatures we shared air space with and explored a lot of territory new to us, we had discovered that Kirby, *Chance Along*, and I were becoming a very capable team.

Brian and Anne became our most frequent guests aboard *Chance Along*, as friends and as charterers. For the first few outings, the trip out to Moho or Birthday Cay was the venue, starting early and motoring from Punta Gorda's Texaco dock. Snorkeling, swimming, dinghy sailing and eating, followed by a breezy downwind sail in the late afternoon, made for a good day. But this trip was to be different.

They and a friend arrived at New Haven aboard Carroll's skiff, *Wiggins*. Once loaded we powered out around Punta Ycacos, went inside McBride Cay and up to Punta Negra to get our northing. A stiff northeast had blown all night, and the sea was rough. We spent the afternoon motor sailing to the Sapodillas. As we came into

the reef area about 4 o'clock, *Chance Along*'s rail went down in a gust and the Perkins lost her prime. Kirby dove into the cabin, somehow managed to put in a new impeller and get the engine going just as we reached Nicolas Cay and its tricky entrance. We dropped sail, and I climbed into the rigging to con us in. The chills and fever I had been experiencing now and again during the week had returned, and I was glad when we entered the basin and I could lie down. We spent a windy night with two anchors dug in by hand; Kirby was anxious about the boat and about me.

The next day was fair and windy. Luckily there was good snorkeling close by. Brian, Anne, and Casper spent the day in the water, rowing the dinghy, exploring the cay, and taking occasional breaks to sunbathe and eat. Except for preparing meals, I spent the day in my bunk; Kirby did dishes, served food and tried to see that everyone was happy. They were the perfect guests, gracious and easy to be with, accepting the prevailing conditions, and Kirby's decisions as captain; they were experienced enough to never ask the impossible. Though I wasn't well enough to participate, in the evening I heard mellow singing, Kirby reciting some of his sailing poems, and friendly relaxed conversation.

We always tried to convey to our guests how we saw this complex environment—how we were attempting to live within its cycles and how it felt when we were successful. Brian and Anne were people who understood our motivation for being out on the water. Anne had grown up sailing and she reveled in the glory of the sea and the sun. For Brian, a geologist, every beach offered a wealth of answers and an equal number of questions to challenge his inquisitive mind. Kirby found him examining the mud on the anchor with a magnifying glass. We had only thought of the seabed in relation to how well the anchor would hold, but Brian was looking for fossils and soil structure that he could read like a history book.

As the tropical dawn came, the guests were in the water swimming to shore for a jog along the beach. On the cay the caretaker's coffee, perking over an open fire, wafted its wonderful aroma out to *Chance Along*. I set a thermos of my own brew on deck and began breakfast, chills and fever gone for the moment.

Breakfast was cleared away, the dinghy was rigged for sailing and the guests went exploring out along the reef. Meanwhile we prepared for getting underway; the second anchor was hauled aboard, lashed in its proper place, and all the loose gear was stowed. When the sun was high enough for good visibility Kirby blew the conch horn to bring them back aboard.

We passed north of the hook in the reef and then on a westerly course toward Punta Gorda. About ten miles farther on, we sailed into a large pod of spotted dolphins. They are smaller than the bottlenose, are extremely fast, and their games are very complex. After waiting in turn, one from each side of the boat would shoot forward, cross the stem and then continue weaving back and forth until another pair took their place. They kept it up for twenty minutes or so.

We had a nice point of sail on the northeast breeze and *Chance Along* ate up the thirty-five miles quickly. In late evening we streaked in under full sail, luffed up into the wind and dropped anchor fifty yards from the Texaco dock.

With no wind or wave protection, unloading was often the hardest part of any Punta Gorda trip. In the stiff evening breeze guests had to be transferred from the rolling deck of *Chance Along* into the wildly pitching dinghy. There was plenty of potential for accidents, but Brian and Anne were veterans and knew the routine. Kirby would stand forward in the dinghy, and Anne would place her right foot on the center thwart, her left in the bottom of the dinghy and quickly plop her fanny on the aft seat. Brian did the same up forward. The second trip Kirby carried Casper and the ice chest.

This time I hardly remembered the passage back, off-loading the guests or even getting ashore myself. I recall how wonderful Christie's hammock felt and how tenderly she nursed me. Sometime in the night she popped a pill in my mouth, "It must be malaria," I heard her tell Kirby.

"We'll get a blood test in the morning; after a week of chloroquin she should feel better."

I dreamed I was with the dolphins crossing and weaving on the bow wave. At first I was watching from the deck and then miraculously I was one of them—swirling through the water, racing to the bow, waiting in line for another turn, in sync with my companions; I was experiencing the natural harmony within this watery world. It was an exhilarating experience. When I woke my mind was confused.

"How are you feeling, Love?"

"I'll be all right." I mumbled. "The dolphins are with me."

Though hard work, chartering allowed us to share our world. We also had the opportunity for experiences beyond measure. Seeing this world through others eyes kept our perspective fresh. Some were more receptive than others to the influence of this experience but almost all received something and felt their lives were richer for having boarded *Chance Along*.

34

~~~

1993—1996

LIVING LIKE A KING

"You live like a king!" That was Frank's comment when I told him what we had been doing with the boat. He had built a furniture business from the proceeds of his VOA construction contract and was doing quite well, but he occasionally chafed under the responsibility of keeping it all going. His statement didn't require an answer, but it gave me something to think about.

For those who watched us sail off on a sunny afternoon, our life might have appeared idyllic, but that was far from the truth. After a day's exposure to the elements, we bathed in the breezy cockpit using a scant amount of fresh water, then slept in sometimes-rolly bunks. We lived without refrigeration, and since we moved at the speed of a fast walk, we spent hours traveling just to obtain basic supplies. Challenging, yes, exciting at times and often rewarding, but our lives were definitely not idyllic.

We worked hard to remain afloat, in every sense of the word. Chartering and dinghy building had broadened our earning base, but the upgrading and maintenance costs of *Chance Along* soaked up every extra dollar we made. Yet, in a few ways, we did live like royalty: we had a lot of

---

control over how we spent our time, and we were able to make our own decisions. Living at sea was continuing a metamorphosis that Nature had begun in the forest. We were aware that our experiences on the water were changing us, and maybe that was what Frank was alluding to. In some ways we were becoming more like the *cays people* who had characteristics we admired.

Cays people was our term for a type of Belizean and was not limited to those who actually lived on islands. They were people whose lives were closely associated with the sea and it included the crews of the sand-hauling lighters, the tugboat operators, the smack fishermen, those who lived in isolated coastal villages, and the many others whose characters were shaped by this saltwater environment.

For those willing to brave the shoals and reefs, these waters have provided protection from the strength of the sea and sometimes from the might of the law. Pirates and buccaneers used Belize as a base to prey on Spanish galleons, and in hard times, some of them became wood cutters and began harvesting timber. Over the succeeding centuries, countless tons of logwood and mahogany were shipped out to foreign ports. In the late 18th century, a Spanish fleet was sent to dislodge the Belize settlers from territory that Spain claimed. The unexpected resistance from the *baymen* contributed to the fleet's doom but so did the inability to maneuver their ships in the unfamiliar and treacherous waters. Now the mahogany and logwood are gone, the Spanish don't invade as a military force, and the pirating is less overt, but the sea remains the same.

Protected water is a relative term. Though ocean waves rarely penetrate the reef, strong winds can generate steep, breaking waves. These conditions, when combined with the underwater hazards, can make this a dangerous place in which to travel. Those who live and work in these waters have great respect for the sea and plan their activities around its moods. Additionally, they use Nature's forces to their advantage as much as possible.

Before we built *Chance Along,* Tina and I were on our way to Belize City in *Sunalee* to distribute a month's production of craft items. It was early January and a cold front dominated the weather. In contrast to the northerly winds that prevail in Belize City during these systems, a southwest wind frequently blows in the southern part of the country. We jumped on it and let it carry us up the coast to Placencia where it gave way to its cold northwesterly brother.

The next sixty miles were hard fought as we worked our way toward our destination. But with the wind blowing off the land, the sea close to shore was fairly smooth and even the little 22-footer could make progress. On the fifth day out, we were in sight of the city and were congratulating ourselves on our sailing skills. West of us were three sailing lighters that had loaded sand near the mouth of the Sibun River. On the foreshore at Belize City, they would shovel off their loads to be picked up later by trucks. Our course would soon cross theirs, and we shook out the reef in the mains'l in anticipation of joining the convoy.

The first one was the big gaffer *United*, and she passed us 300 yards to windward. The next two were smaller and gunter-rigged, and they sailed by leaving us to wonder if we were stopped at some intersection. Much later we caught up with them at their anchorage and discussions with the sailors provided an explanation. A cold front can produce a two-knot, south-setting current in the channel. The lighters were not only riding a counter current closer to shore, but they had kept a course that gave them a fair wind. We, on the other hand, had chosen the shortest route and were bucking into the wind, the waves, and the current. We were trying to force our way and were making little forward progress.

On our first trip to the southern end of the reef with *Sunalee*, we worked our way through the coral heads and anchored off Lighthouse Cay. Ashore we were greeted by an older couple who we met occasionally in town. Bernard was busy grating coconuts, the first step in making oil. He complimented me on our "pretty yacht." He had traveled by sail during his early years but now had an outboard engine on his dory. The fishing wasn't like it used to be, but they still caught what they needed for the household and had extra to sell in the market when they bought provisions. He asked if I was still making carvings, did they sell well, and how had the wind been on our passage out. It was an easy man-to-man conversation uncluttered by our difference in skin color or by my foreignness; the sea was our common interest.

"I hear on the radio that Mr. George gone," he said.

"You mean George Vernon, Mr. Bernard?"

"Yah, it look like his time come."

George had run the general store where we bought most of our supplies and we considered him a personal friend. Bernard must have known him much better, and I marveled at his seemingly easy acceptance of the loss, but on second thought, exposed to Nature the way he was, death was perhaps as natural as a sunset.

Their children were going to school on the mainland, and Bernard and Pearl stayed on the cay by themselves. Their income came from his stipend as keeper of the lighthouse and his return from the sale of fish, conch, lobster and coconut oil. Periodically they travelled the 35 miles of open water to Punta Gorda in their small boat to sell their products and buy provisions.

An understanding of the clouds, wind, waves, tides and the phase of the moon was essential for their living and travelling, but even more so was self-reliance. Trouble at sea would put their lives in danger and the problem would be theirs alone to solve.

On one of our early trips with *Chance Along*, we got in trouble because of several poor decisions. Christie and Carlos had spent the day with us at New Haven where we fished, collected coconuts, and visited with boating friends. We lost track of the time and started our return trip too late in the afternoon. It was important that they get to their caretaking job that evening, since the owners were leaving in the morning. I decided we could arrive before dark if we hurried along with both motor and sail.

The light faded until I could no longer see the tiny cay I had been using for a reference point. We had made the passage once before, but it was in broad daylight and I had been able to judge our distance from shore. For any sailor, the grating of his keel as it scrapes the bottom is a frightful sound–for me it was painful. We slid to a stop, and then heeled slightly to port. With less than a mile to go, we had hit an isolated shoal. Tina flew to the halyards to get the sails down so the following wind wouldn't force us farther onto the shoal, and I put the motor in reverse with full throttle in a fruitless attempt to back off.

We had occasionally run aground with shallow-draft *Sunalee*, and we knew that eventually it would happen with *Chance Along,* so I had thought through the actions that must be taken. Still, I was unprepared for the almost debilitating emotions that first-grounding engendered. Through my error, she was now lying immobilized and helpless. Though she was not taking on water, I felt guilty, as if I had injured her. Everyone must feel protective of their creations: a poem, sculpture, score of music, an architectural design, or a structure like a boat; but I was reacting to *Chance Along* like she was a living thing, almost as if she were a child I was responsible for.

In the last of the light, we loaded the anchor in the dinghy, and I rowed it out and dropped it 25 yards to windward. Carlos took up the slack with the windlass, while I sounded around the boat with the lead line. The stern was hard aground, but the bow, drawing two feet less, was still afloat. Carlos put all his strength into the windlass but the bow only turned a little toward the deeper water before the anchor started dragging. As darkness fell, the wind decreased, and we considered alternatives; Carlos suggested putting the ballast overboard in an orderly fashion so it could be recovered later, but it would probably only raise the boat an inch or two and we were stuck fast. If I understood the displacement principle correctly, it would be more effective to move the ballast within the boat; lowering the bow should cause the stern to rise. So by using the bucket brigade method, we shifted a thousand pounds of lead bars from amidships to the forepeak sole.

Carlos went back to work at the windlass while the rest of us put our weight as far forward as possible by scooting out on the bowsprit. Gradually she turned, and at last we floated free. We felt our way offshore and anchored for the night.

Euphoria kept me awake and made me wonder if I was manic-depressive. My error in judgment hadn't been erased, in fact it was indelibly chalked on my memory's slate, but it had led to a worthwhile experience. Even without a helpful tide or a tugboat, we had recovered from a serious grounding by using our wits to take advantage of the natural law of flotation. It seemed as if we had passed some test—that we were now qualified to be out there.

The techniques we had been learning, sailing, boat handling, navigation and fishing, had been new to us—rightfully so, since neither of us grew up around water. But it seemed the basics of living with Nature were lessons we should already have known. We have tried to adopt a set of guidelines:

1. Use resources sustainably or they will run out.

2. Don't interfere with natural cycles—they are what keep the whole system functioning.

3. Respect all the other members of creation, keeping in mind that Man is only one player in Nature's large team.

4. Death is just as essential as birth—learn to accept it.

Somehow during our culture's evolution, these fundamentals were lost from the curriculum; perhaps they were imagined to be obsolete. Having control of our immediate environment leads to the illusion we control Nature herself. I was quickly disabused of that idea the first time *Chance Along* was tossed about by wind and waves. The sea is governed by a system that is powerful beyond comprehension—one in which we don't have a vote—it is only natural to ally ourselves with those forces in an effort to survive. Perhaps this explains the special type of humility, characterized by those who travel the sea in small boats.

I wanted to laugh thinking of Frank's comment about living like a king. If he could only see me now! What king would have to scrub the bottom of his carriage? I surfaced, blasted the water out of my snorkel and took a gulp of air. After being disturbed from their shelters in the slime, the miniature shrimp were seeking new homes and several dozen seemed to have found haven in my ears and body hair, their wriggling adding discomfort to an already unpleasant job. But I was accustomed to its periodic necessity and now I found humor in it. At the moment the only nobility I might even faintly resemble was that fabled emperor—the one who wore no clothes.

35
~~~

1993—1996 . . . . . .

LINES TO WRITE AND SPLICE

Kirby rowed out from the New Haven shop, dusted off his clothes and climbed aboard. Lunch was ready, and I had hung the red towel in the rigging to notify him.
"What color is bismuth?" he asked.
"Why are you asking?"
"Well, I was trying to describe a certain color of blue, probably *cerulean*, but it wrecks the alliteration; *bismuth* sounds better."
He handed me a scrap of well-used sand paper with a penciled verse on the back.

> *'Candescent clouds and gliding gulls,*
> *The sea a magic mirror*
> *That cat's paws swipe to bismuth blue,*
> *As turquoise trades draw nearer.*

Kirby had kept a trip diary during our various travels, but when we started the boatbuilding, he began a daily journal. He not only included the many steps of the process he was working through but had notations of our activities, what we were currently reading, rhymes, puns, our health status and the evolving local and international political scenes—a real potpourri. But the poetry was something new.

Sporadically I have kept diaries and journals, handwritten pages describing my transformations from traditional wife and mother to independent woman, California gal to world citizen, and forest dweller to sea gypsy. They serve as a running dialogue with myself concerning the ups and downs of daily life in this wild place. My idealism often trips me up as I grapple with the real world, and I use writing as a way to regain my footing.

To paint scenes with words—that's what we found ourselves trying to do—Kirby with verses that popped into his mind at odd moments and me with essays, short stories, and now and then, a poem. Though inspired writing was not new to either of us, the amount that was pouring out was a surprise. It was as if we had tapped into a new creative source and the words were flowing forth.

Necessity made Belize a fertile ground for imaginative thinking. An intimate understanding and respect for the natural environment were requirements for those who lived in the forest. Just living at this fundamental level was a creative act. We arrived with basic skills, a willingness to work and the desire to learn. Fate had set us down in an area with creative fires all around us—it wasn't so much a match that put our tinder ablaze, it was more like spontaneous combustion. Since we had arrived in Belize with so little, we too had necessity to encourage us; we had to have shelter and a way of making a living. This had carried us through the tree house construction and the development of our craft business. The building of *Chance Along* also had the element of need since having her was a requirement for fulfilling our dream.

But the sea environment's vastness and constant changeableness has stirred something deeper—the need for soul-level expression. Now we create without being required to do so. We feel motivated to put our new experiences into words so that we might better understand them, and we want to share our insights with others. Sensing all life is regulated by Nature's rhythms, both externally and internally, we are, at times, fully tuned to our environment, and we experience a kind of resonance that fuels our creativity. We find excitement in exploring both Nature's harmonic and our new talents.

I AM

the arms that enfold the child and lift the load
the hands that knead and pat the tortillas in daily cycles
the lips that kiss the brow and sip the bubbling broth on the
fire
the skin that tingles to a stroke.

I am
the eyes that see the soaring frigate riding thermals in an
azure sky
the nose that smells advancing rain in flits and flurries,
gusts and gushes, walls of water
the ears that hear whispering air and rumbling thunder
the tongue that tastes the wild wind.

I am
the cheek that presses rough tree bark and the smooth stone
the fingers that feel the moss and pluck the golden plum
the toes that grip the soil, squish the mud, and reshape the
sand
the eyelash where the dewdrop lingers.

I am
the mind that imagines the wind on the wings of the falcon
and follows the fable
the intuition that lurks behind lace, sorting shifting
shadows
the heart that beats the rhythms of passing time
the waxing and waning of the moon.

I am woman.

CLS

OF REEFS AND WARBLERS

I am sitting on deck watching the sun rise over the reef extending left and right as far as the eye can see. With nothing above the surface between us and that wall of pounding surf a few hundred yards away, we feel the full force of the wind and a moderate swell at our anchorage. The feeling of vulnerability encourages contemplation.

A small warbler perched under the boom saddle. It rested fifteen minutes or so and then flew west, the same direction it had come from though the nearest land is twenty miles away. It arrived and departed as a courier might, but since it didn't warble anything I am left to wonder what message he might have had for me.

A half mile away, I can see the partially completed concrete retaining walls and stone cabanas on tiny Tom Owens Cay. Yesterday the caretaker gave us a tour and a description of the building plan. When it is completed the cay will be, in essence, man-made. The man doing the building is a gringo like me, with a stated goal to "enhance Nature." A year ago the only residents of this tiny spit of sand and coconuts were sea birds, and occasionally, camping fishermen. Why do people of my culture, maybe all cultures, have this adversarial relationship with Nature—almost an adolescent type of defiance—as if we weren't part of it? I feel it in myself, at times, and it is apparent in almost all the activities of Western culture. We call it "development," a concept which has, for most people, positive connotations but often has long-term negative effects on the environment.

The original falling out with God may have happened long before the apple incident. Perhaps Adam began building a stone wall around the Garden. He probably thought it looked better, or maybe it was to keep the 'possums out of the pineapples. Whatever the reason, Adam thought it was a sign of progress and called it development, though in reality, it was an act of arrogance. Man has been trying to improve on Nature ever since.

Historically, humankind has been aware of this perverse competition with God's other creatures, as well as the tendency to show disrespect for His craftsmanship. Aware and worried enough, humans developed Religion as a formula to excuse their actions—complete with a set of rules that, if followed, allow them to continue their arrogant and destructive ways and even be rewarded for it in the hereafter. Religion also serves as a narcotic that keeps humans from recognizing the many signs that indicate that God is really losing patience.

I wonder about my role in this scenario. I really can't accept the concept that someone has already taken the rap for me so I don't have to take responsibility for the effect of my actions on my fellow creatures. My mom told me when I threw my gum wrapper on the ground that the whole world would become a mound of trash if everyone did that. I picked it up and have tried not to live a life of littering. In addition, I try to chew no more than my share of the world's gum. At that, I am only partly successful.

It is a rewarding experience to observe, from a fragile boat, waves breaking on a nearby reef. It restrains one's arrogant tendencies. I also spend a lot of time looking at sunrises and listening to little birds, as if in them I will find some answers.

KGS

BREATHING BOND

The sea, though calm, retains the will
To act as Nature's giant still,
And thus sublimes those near to me:
The dolphin, the turtle and the manatee.

As we together share the air
I deeply sense a bond is there;
For by nature we accept as kin
Those we hear breathe out and in.

So if we could hone our listening sense
Then few need flee from our offense;
And wouldn't all then gain reprieve,
For doesn't every creature breathe?

KGS

HARVEST CAY DOLPHIN

Here she comes—a shadow beneath the water's surface streaking toward the bow of my little ship. Her streamlined shape aligns itself just below the stem, undulating with the bow wave. After a moment she moves to starboard, her bulbous head rising above the water, her blow hole spouting—whoosh. Her eye seems to survey Chancy and me, and then she is beneath the surface again, moving under the stem in her graceful dance.

I watch, struck with longing, awe and gratitude that she has come to play with *Chance Along*. Lying down, level with the deck, I watch intently. She surfaces again, and again we connect eye to eye. She stays with us a quarter mile, abruptly swerving off to port. *Chance Along* continues on her way through the shoals toward our anchorage.

I observe the evening's progression as I come from below. The sun sinks behind the mountains as clouds build over the western horizon, the wind sings through the rigging, and the waves slap the hull. We are tucked securely behind Harvest Cay where I see the lights of Placencia come on one after another. In the quiet she is suddenly there, surfacing just beside me, my water world friend, her white scar evident in the dim light.

"Hello," I softly call and she dives. Circling, coming, going, coming, she surfaces beside *Chance Along* and I know she knows I wait for her. Her circles slowly expand out farther and farther; the night drops its curtain and I can no longer see her. But I hold her in my mind's eye, a friend who came and filled my need when my heart called.

CLS

36

~~~

Fall 1996

WHAT STORM?

The tiny flashlight on my forehead picks up the raindrops just before they slam into my face. They are blown out of the void like ink drops, but pushed by forty knots of wind, they sting like pellets. My foul-weather gear breaks the wind but does little to keep the rain out, and my clothes are soaked through. Tina is even more exposed up on the bow, and I fear for her safety as *Chance Along* pitches with the breaking waves. She signals me to give the engine more throttle to ease the tension on the anchor line.

Last evening we arrived here at Columbus Cay, a short distance from Belize's barrier reef, after a glorious ten-mile sail. We dropped anchor on a sandy flat west of the cay where we were protected from the easterly trade wind. I donned mask and fins and set the anchor by hand, but the underlying hard coral shoal prevented the fluke from digging in deeply. We had a light supper in the cockpit, relaxing in that enjoyably-tired way that comes after a successful workout. When we went to our bunks, the sky was clear and the great hunter Orion had just raised his club above the horizon, perhaps as a warning signal.

We had noticed lightning flashes in the Maya Mountains to the southwest, but in October, thunderstorms from that quadrant are uncommon, and we are ten miles from the mainland where they spawn. But in the eight hours after sundown it had come—the dreaded biama. After a brief calm, the wind had shifted 180 degrees, and now the cay is a hazard.

The storm winds continue to wail unabated. In the lightning flashes, I can make out the silhouette of the palm trees, only two dozen yards on our stern; they don't seem to be getting closer. I check the lead line I have draped over the rail. With the help of the diesel engine ticking over at a fast idle, the anchor has held but I know our situation is perilous.

During *Chance Along*'s construction, we dreamed of learning the seasonal cycles and the patterns of the wind, waves, and sea life in Belize's coastal waters. It would be an exercise similar to our study of the forest, we reasoned. This notion was quickly dispelled. Granted, the forest and the creatures that inhabit it have a powerful persistence, and it is easy to believe that when Man is gone the forest will reclaim its original territory—one only needs to witness an unexcavated Mayan site to observe this phenomenon. But with only basic tools, machete, axe, and fire, Man can manipulate or even destroy forests. The sea, on the other hand, refuses domination, and this difference in character is immediately apparent to those who attempt to learn its ways.

Even in calm water, a person aboard a small sailing vessel senses the immense power of the sea. It toys with *Chance Along*'s nine tons as if they were nothing; even a wavelet will cause a little pitch or roll. Under the vast dome of the sky, winds will be created—winds that can vary from gentle breezes to hurricanes but winds that no man will influence. There is a sensation of vastness, of unfathomable power and an indifference that is not felt in the forest. Feeling more humble than bold, a wise mariner petitions to participate in this magnificence, never demands.

The stakes are higher here—the risks and also the rewards. Our choices can make the difference between an exhilarating experience and a miserable and frightening one; on rare occasions a poor choice could lead to the destruction of our vessel and physical harm to her crew. We must analyze the natural patterns of the sea even more diligently than we did the forest. Clouds: the puffy cumulus, the anvil-shaped thunderheads or the high wispy cirrus, inform us about local and regional weather systems. The waves often foretell the strength and direction of the winds that will follow, winds whose patterns vary between locations. Because of the complex interaction of the elements, the study becomes as much an art as a science and we learn to rely on our intuition as the final arbiter in decision making.

With a flash of lightning and a simultaneous clap of deafening thunder, the skies over us open in a drenching downpour. Soon the wind starts dropping, and temporarily blinded, I grope for the clutch lever to avoid overrunning the anchor line. I signal to Tina to return to the relative safety of the cockpit. Using the hand rails she works her way aft over the wildly-pitching side deck. We hold each other for a moment in the way that only reunited lovers can—the deluge pouring over us being of little concern.

In a few minutes, the rain subsides, the wind drops below ten knots and starts veering to the north. I kill the diesel, pick up the lead, check the anchor line, shuck off my sodden clothes, and climb down into the cabin. Tina already has the kettle on, and after drinking a cup of Milo and donning dry underwear we collapse in exhausted sleep.

The sun climbs the coconut palms as if in search of a morning toddy, then on up into a cloudless sky. A gentle breeze is already moving from north to east in its preparation for the day's work. Few words are exchanged as we sip our morning coffee, but our feeling of bliss is tangible. We treasure the moment as our reward for the hour-long minutes we spent just hoping we would survive the night. Tina sighs, "I really felt like *Chance Along* was taking care of us as much as we were of her."

"I was sending her encouragement, something like, 'We're all in this together. You must do your part.'"

Both Tina and I had sensed a growing presence during the construction process. Now as our sailing experiences accumulate, we realize that *Chance Along* has developed a fully fledged personality of her own. In the days of working sail, crew members would, after spending months aboard, assign a personality to their ship. It would be related to her sailing characteristics but also to something less definable—her luck.

The fact that we are here enjoying the morning sun is confirmation enough that *Chance Along* is a lucky ship. Some of our success in surviving the storm could be credited to the actions of her crew but some was due to *Chancy's* personal characteristics. She kept her bow facing into even the strongest of the storm gusts, thus presenting the least resistance. Had she veered off broadside to the wind, as so many boats would have, the motor wouldn't have helped her and the strain on the anchor lines would have been greatly increased. If she was the type to plunge off the wave crests, surely she would have been slamming her keel on the bottom with so little water under her. Yes, she did her part well.

In general we have tried to take a page from the old schoonermen's log book, not only in the name we gave our vessel, but in their philosophy. It is said those captains didn't risk their cargos, vessels, and crew if they could possibly avoid it; they found shelter and held back for better weather conditions—they waited their *chance along*. But avoiding storms is not always possible, as we found out during the night. In choosing to propel our vessel by sail, we put ourselves at the mercy of the wind and the sea. At the same time there is great satisfaction in being able to use these forces to reach our destination, so we strive to fashion a working relationship with them.

We have land where we can build a house; there, we could just close the shutters during a storm and return to a warm, dry bed. Even if we want to continue living aboard, we could stay in a good anchorage or even go up the Rio Dulce and live in a marina. There were times in the night when these options seemed very attractive, but my perspective has brightened with the rising of the sun and undoubtedly has become less rational. Now the storm is over and we are safe; I feel lucky to be where I am. We have faced a dangerous situation and in surviving have gained confidence. But I am also left with a sensation less easily described. It is a good feeling, one of security that comes from knowing we are a part of something omnipotent.

We have learned enough of the natural patterns out here to feel that we have carved a little niche for ourselves and that fosters a certain joy that we experience nowhere else. But since what we *don't know* is immense, there is an ever-present challenge to continue learning. Moreover, there is a certain appeal to the risk taking, and like any form of gambling, sailing has an addictive element.

"The pancakes are good."

She always tells me that, even though I know she must get tired of them morning after morning. It is my one contribution to our onboard cuisine.

"Are you ready to cross over to Long Cay?"

"Sure, those guys just did it. But it looks pretty tricky."

She is referring to the fishing smack that has just gone by a few hundred yards to the west. It is an area thick with coral heads but those fishermen know the waters and probably only draw three feet. A few hours rest after a terrible night and she is ready for the next adventure— what a woman! Maybe it was worth the frightening experience just to be reminded how lucky I am to have her by my side.

The anchor comes up so easily, I know it had barely been holding during the storm. We start picking our way through the minefield of coral. It will be a mile or more before we reach the main channel. Luckily the water is clear, and the sun is high enough so Tina, up in the ratlines, can see a good distance in front and also down into the water and estimate the depth of the heads. She directs me with hand signals. I am giving instructions to *Chance Along* with the tiller and the trim of the sails. *Chancy,* with a tug at the tiller, a flutter of her sail, or the angle of her deck, reports back to me, the wind and sea conditions and her opinion of my boat handling skills. It's a team effort and we depend on each other.

The pelicans have had their breakfast and we left them bathing near the cay. Four or five frigatebirds are soaring over us and there are probably many more up beyond my vision. My skin tingles with the contrasting sensations of the sun's warmth and the coolness of the morning breeze, and I feel fully alive. A quiet symphony is playing as the chirp of a soaring osprey, the splash of a diving tern, and the creak of the swinging boom add melody to the background murmur of the distant reef as *Chance Along*'s bow parts the crystal water.

Today's panorama varies with every point of the compass: the turquoise waters with brown and yellow coral patches, the endless sliver of white foam on the reef, our red masthead pennant, as it reaches toward the cotton clouds of an azure sky, the waving palm trees on nearby cays, and the backdrop of the verdant mountain range. A sharp lookout, on a day like today, might even glimpse tomorrow—another day of promise.

BIAMA
To the south the stars are gone;
Now hear the grumbling thunder;
The blackness spawns to form a void
That lightning splits asunder.

In ominous calm warm winds are gone
And left us all alone,
'Til cold puffs come like the breath of death
And chill us to the bone.

The scope is out, the awning down,
The biama starts to blow;
Our faith now lies in our little ship
As she turns to face the foe.

The rigging's whine becomes a howl;
To survive is now our goal,
As lightning blinds my anxious eyes
And thunder slams my soul.

Finally comes the pelting rain
That calms the screaming beast;
To sleep we crash on welcome bunks
As stars show west and east.

Why subject one's self to such a night
So far beyond the norm?
As the sweet breeze wafts the golden dawn
My answer is "What storm?"

KGS

GLOSSARY

Abeam or **on the beam**: referring to the wind coming toward the side of the boat.

Back: to hold the sail so it will fill on the opposite side.

Biama: a brief but violent thunder storm usually originating in the southern quadrant.

Come about: to turn the bow across the wind onto the other tack.

Gaff: a short spar that supports the upper edge of a sail.

Jib: a small triangular sail in front of the forward mast.

Jibe: a shift of the boom from one side to the other while sailing downwind.

Kriol: an African-Belizean of mixed blood.

Lead line: a weighted line used to determine water depths.

Luff: to allow the wind to spill out of the sail.

Ogee: a decorative "S" shaped molding.

Reef: to reduce the sail area by tying a portion of it to the boom.

Sand lighter: a sailing vessel that carries construction sand from the river mouths.

Scope: the length of the anchor line.

Sea breeze: a cooling breeze that blows inland from the sea.

Sheer line: the curve in the uppermost plank of a vessel.

Smack: a sailing vessel used for fishing (originally with a well amidships to keep the fish alive).

Stays'l: an additional triangular sail hoisted forward of a mast.

Tack: to turn the bow across the wind and proceed along the course in a zigzag manner.

ACKNOWLEDGEMENTS

Many friends and acquaintances went out of their way to give support and encouragement during the years it took to build our vessel and we want to thank them all. A list would fill a book of its own, but there were those who travelled the "extra mile:" Christie and Carlos Juarez, K. Scott Salisbury, Russ Salisbury, Ron Chingery, John Spang, Hal Palmer, Dale and Eleanor Lanyon, Robert and Lou Nicolait, Kerfoot Walker, Melvin Pemberton, Frank Dirhotto, Dave Johnson, and Jim and Gae MacDonald. It is impossible to express enough appreciation to each of these deserving people. Some part of their spirit sails with us each time we weigh *Chance Along's* anchor.

We want to express thanks to those who have helped in the creation of this book: Tanya Russ, Christie Juarez, Bob Stoddard, and Lou Nicolait. Each has given their time and perspective, making this book better than it would have been otherwise.

In 1972, Kirby and Christina Salisbury set aside their jobs in California to have a tropical experience with their young children. The adventure, intended to last no more than two years, has not yet ended. They operated a woodcraft/boatbuilding business for 25 years and have sailed Belize's complex waters for 40.

Recently they have taken on the challenge of creative writing and in 2009, *Treehouse Perspectives: Living High on Little* was published.

They continue to live aboard their schooner (the launch of this book celebrates *Chance Along's* 25th anniversary). They love to hear from their readers and can be contacted via *biamabooks@gmail.com.*

Made in the USA
Lexington, KY
22 March 2014